Country modern

Country modern

Author Aurora Cuito

Editor Paco Asensio

Translation Wendy Griswold

Art director Mireia Casanovas Soley

Graphic design and layout Emma Termes Parera

2001 © Loft Publications S.L. and HBI,
an imprint of HarperCollins Publishers

First published in 2001 by LOFT and HBI,
an imprint of HarperCollins Publishers
10 East 53rd St. New York, NY 10022-5299

Distributed in the U.S and Canada by Watson-Guptill Publications
770 Broadway New York, NY 10003-9595
Telephone: (800) 451-1741 or (732) 363-4511 in NJ, AK, HI
Fax: (732) 363-0338

Distributed throughout the rest of the world by
HarperCollins International
10 East 53rd St. New York, NY 10022-5299
Fax: (212) 207-7654

Hardcover ISBN 0-06-621363-0
Softcover ISBN 0-8230-0967-X

Printed in Spain

Introduction

These days, building in the countryside raises many architectural problems and paradoxes. The designers featured in this book have been able to address the special needs created by climate and topography, as well as the clients' requests, in grand style.

Various parameters come together in the houses we have selected. The architects use new techniques and recently-marketed industrial products along with typical construction details and components as historically important as wood and stone. So the houses have a contemporary look while echoing architectural tradition and including elements evocative of the old indigenous farms.

The setting is enormously significant in determining the end result of the projects, serving not only as a framework for the architecture, but

also imposing certain requirements. As far as the climate is concerned, factors such as humidity, temperature changes, or snow require solid buildings with high thermal inertia for energy efficiency: retaining heat in winter and cool air in summer.

Integrating the building into the surroundings is another challenge the architects faced: not disguising the structure amid the foliage or blending in the materials found in the countryside, but paying tribute to nature. Some of the homes presented here are built into the ground, hiding themselves amid the hills; others sit on platforms to smooth out uneven plots and enjoy extensive views; but all change the landscape only to enhance it.

Modern country houses presents a carefully-chosen selection of homes that exemplify this meeting of man and nature, architect and landscape, the vernacular and the modern.

The meeting of man and nature produces architecture that enhances its setting

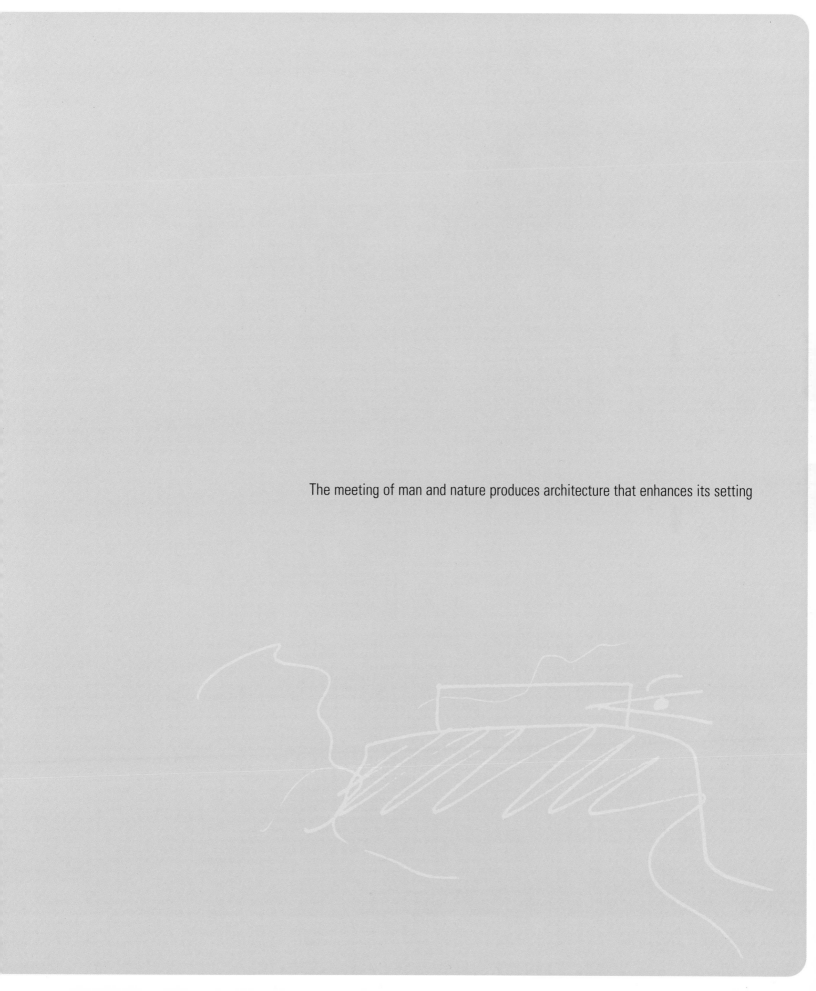

Photographs: **Ignacio Martínez**

Kaufmann House

Hermann Kaufmann

Collaborators: **Stefan Hiebeler and Anton Kaufmann**   Construction date: **1998**   Location: **Reuthe, Austria**   Area: **3900 sq. feet**

In recent years, the tiny region of Vorarlberg, in northern Austria, has witnessed the burgeoning of a new environmentally friendly, sustainable architecture which respects the magnificent landscape and is simultaneously influenced by a deeply-rooted tradition of handicrafts and the latest advances in construction techniques. Thanks to these qualities and the expertise of Austrian architects, the area is setting an excellent precedent for designers in other parts of the world.

In this special environment, Hermann Kaufmann, an architect who has enjoyed a brilliant professional career, was chosen to build a house for the owner of a lumber company - which explains the selection of wood as the predominant material.

The home consists of two sections placed perpendicularly on a slight slope. The socle acts as a transition between the domestic spaces and the lot. It is dug partially into the ground and, since it serves as the building's structural base, the concrete is exposed. It houses the garage, several service rooms, and a storage area.

The upper level, perpendicular to the slope, is long and rises above the solid block like a balcony reaching out toward the magnificent Austrian countryside. A distance of 7 meters was required between the northern and southern facades, so the structure was designed with double T-shaped beams, 30 cm high. This floor, which includes all the domestic rooms, is accessed by narrow wooden stairs supported by metal cylinders which are anchored in the framework of the upper level and also serve as handrails.

The northern, eastern, and western facades were constructed with boards made from three layers of larch wood, guaranteeing good thermal isolation. The joints between the boards are covered with long aluminum sheets that keep the building watertight. The southern façade, almost entirely glass, is protected by sliding blinds installed a short distance from the large windows. The space in between functions as a small balcony. The blinds can be moved as desired in accordance with the season or time of day.

The roofs of the two sections are basically flat, with a slight slope for drainage. A fine covering of gravel and earth conceals the asphalt and insulating material. The local climate has encouraged the growth of a layer of grass, making the roof blend in with the landscape.

Inside, the vertical surfaces are covered with wood, the typical finish of houses in the region

Despite its contemporary design, the house, built into the ground and making heavy use of wood, blends in with the magnificent landscape.

The owner of the house was also the builder. His lumber company provided the material and furnished specific information about complicated construction details.

The staircase is a magnificent piece of construction. Thin metal cylinders anchored in the framework of the upper level support the wooden stairs, which also rest on a steel column.

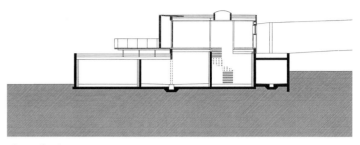

Western Elevation

Cross-Section

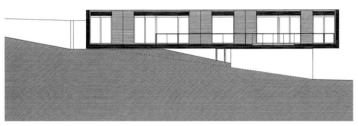

Southern elevation

1. Garage   7. Corridor
2. Storage areas   8. Kitchen
3. Office   9. Study
4. Laundry room   10. Living room
5. Walk-in closet   11. Bedroom
6. Bathrooms   12. Sauna

N

First floor

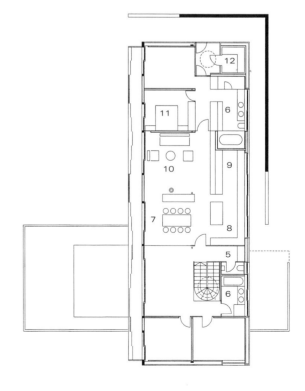

Second floor

15

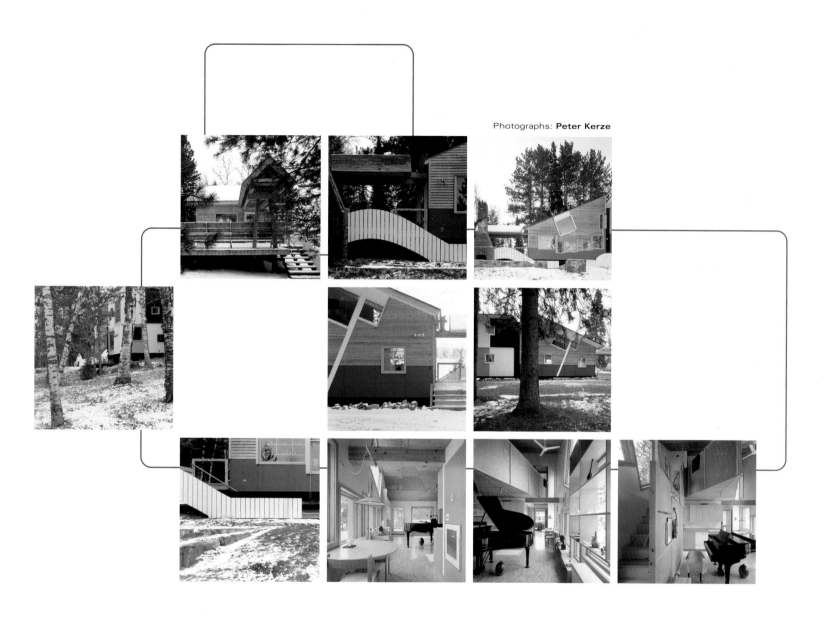

Photographs: **Peter Kerze**

Lutz House

David Salmela

Construction date: **1998**   Location: **Duluth, Minnesota, USA**   Area: **1095 sq. feet**

One of the challenges an architect faces when he designs a house is assimilating his clients' needs and satisfying them using a language all his own. In this project, David Salmela did not have to deal with whims and demands, because the owners participated actively in the design process and were bold enough to take their chances with the riskiest proposals.

The house is on a lake near Duluth, Minnesota, in an area where Swedish immigrant families who retained the custom of enjoying a second residence far from the urban hustle and bustle used to spend their summers. The family owned the original building, which was in poor condition and was torn down. The foundations and the old fireplace were retained for sentimental reasons, and the new house was built behind them, closer to the water.

The building is long and narrow, with magnificent views and abundant natural light. It consists of a cube that houses several rooms on two floors, and a two-story living room. The rooms are open and can be used for different purposes.

The exterior spaces were carefully designed for enjoyment of outdoor activities. There are two routes to the lake: around the ruins or directly from the house, across a porch that provides shade in the summer.

The house's wooden structure is supported by a system of concrete pillars that raise it above ground level, protecting it from dampness. The exterior walls are cedar and painted plywood, and the interior is pine. Some of the furnishings, like those in the kitchen, and most of the closets, are built into the walls. Out of a deep concern for the ecology, the architect and clients made sure that no materials harmful to the environment were used.

The electrical and mechanical systems were installed between the floor and the ground, so they would be accessible but out of the way of any household activity.

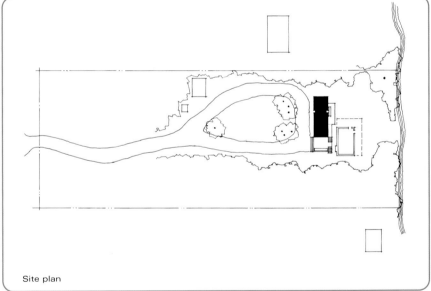

Site plan

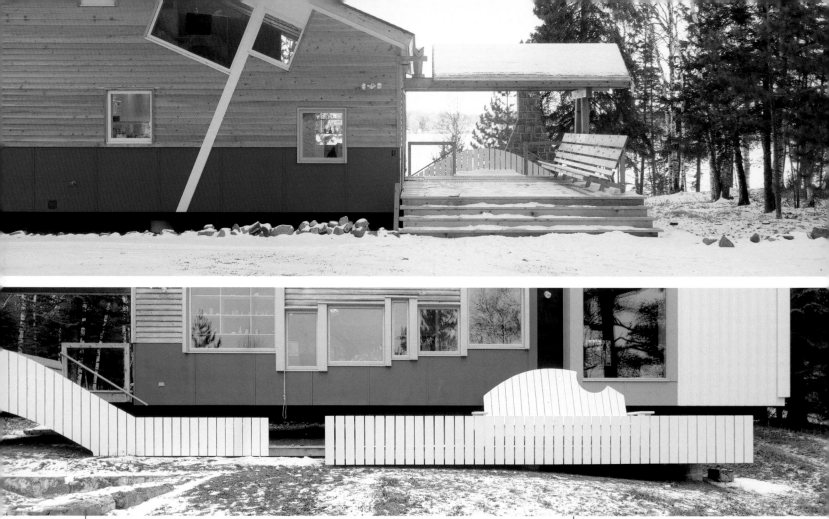

The house has contemporary architectural lines with subtle classical references. It is both rustic and unconventional. These recurring paradoxes make for an interesting project, full of feeling.

The interior reflects the owners' artistic interests: music, painting, and ceramics.

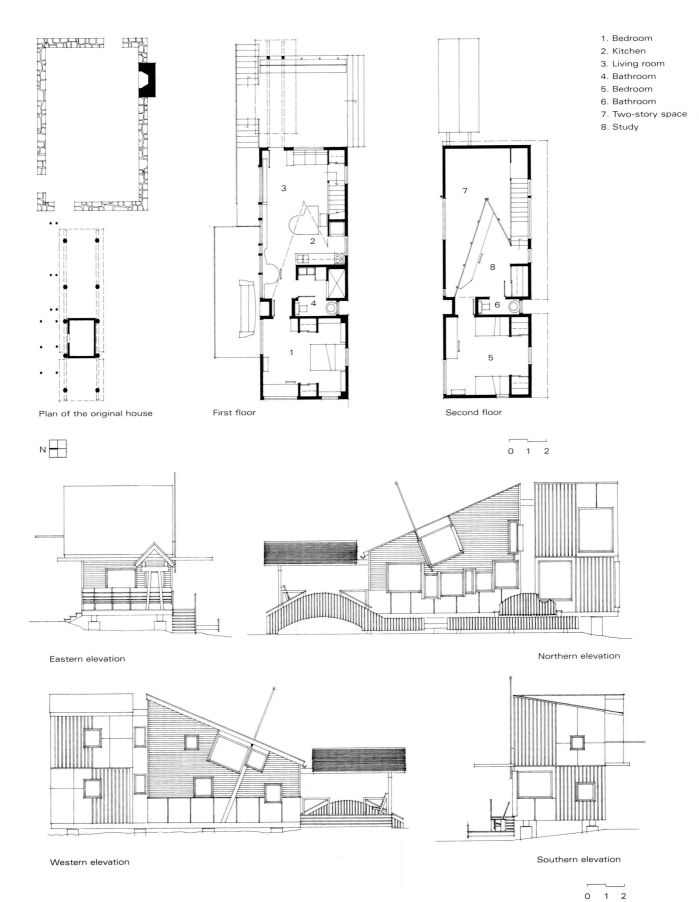

1. Bedroom
2. Kitchen
3. Living room
4. Bathroom
5. Bedroom
6. Bathroom
7. Two-story space
8. Study

Plan of the original house

First floor

Second floor

N

0 1 2

Eastern elevation

Northern elevation

Western elevation

Southern elevation

0 1 2

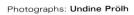

Photographs: **Undine Prölh**

Wood Residence

James Cutler Architects

Construction date: **1997**   Location: **Vashon Island, Washington, USA**   Area: **2320 sq. feet**

The Wood residence is located close to nature, between a lush forest and a grassland with few shrubs. The house is protected by the trees on its northern side, but is exposed on the southern side to take advantage of the clearing's light and views.

Enormous effort was required to satisfy the clients' needs and deal with the features of the land. James Cutler is known for respecting the sites on which he builds, so an important part of the design was an in-depth study of the climate and special characteristics of the plot. In this case, the position of the house and the layout of the rooms were determined by the search for natural light and the desire to retain the existing trees, which stand right near the house.

The residence is comprised of several structures connected by a back hallway that runs its entire length, leveling the slight slopes and leading out to the forest. So the units containing the bedrooms, dayroom, laundry room, greenhouse, and garage are all lined up. The stable and the granary are located a few meters from the residence.

The predominant building material is wood: the vertical interior partitions are panels of pine, the flooring is maple, and the exterior walls are covered with cedar shingles. The only significant amount of metal is in the roof, which is a series of galvanized metal strips. Cutler's dexterity and precision in working the wood are magnificent. The details are visible throughout, and the finishes and structural elements are a lesson in construction in and of themselves.

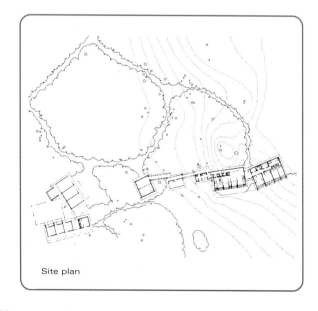

Site plan

The interior is all wood. The furniture, designed by the architects - note the kitchen cupboards and the living room cabinets - were conceived as self-contained modules. Lighting was installed above the furnishings and below the ceiling.

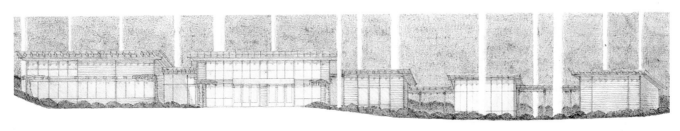

Elevation

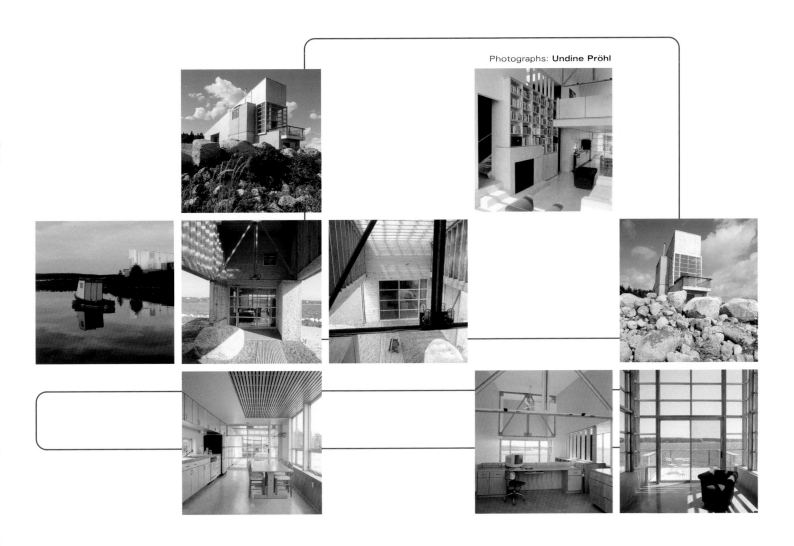

Photographs: **Undine Pröhl**

Howard House

Bryan MacKay-Lyons

Collaborators: **Niall Savage** and **Trevor Davies**   Construction date: **1999**   Location: **West Pennant, Nova Scotia, Canada**   Area: **1950 sq. feet**

The firm headed by Bryan MacKay-Lyons opts for simple but powerful architecture, uncomplicated but striking shapes, which indisputably dominate whatever setting they are placed in. The Howard House, near the coast of Nova Scotia, is one of the best examples of their work.

The project resembles a huge wall housing domestic activities. The facades of this enormous building are covered with corrugated aluminum, galvanized to protect the metal from the rain and sea salt. In contrast to the bucolic surroundings, it has an industrial look to it, yet it is reminiscent of the austere buildings typical of the area.

The reinforced concrete foundations emerge from the ground to form a socle that bears witness to how difficult it is to erect a building in a place where the level of the water table can vary greatly. In addition to this solid concrete plinth, there is a concrete staircase, attached to the main structure, which provides shelter from the icy west winds and thermal isolation for the house.

The roof, which slopes in just one direction, rises toward the south, covering one continuous space that contains, successively, the garage, the patio at the entrance, the kitchen, the living room, and the projecting balcony. Some elements, such as the fireplace, the interior bridge, and the glass-covered southern façade, create interesting shapes and angles, adding small, comfortable areas that enrich the home.

Spatial perceptions in some of the rooms were altered through the use of ceramic tiles on the floors and the lower walls up to the window sills, which also affords a sense of continuity.

The structural skeleton can be seen throughout the house: the metal truss dominates the loft and the wooden frame is exposed in various segments of the ceiling and walls.

The overall result is a practical, sculptural, minimalist work, influenced by the austerity of the local architecture and blending with the setting.

From the outside, the house designed by Bryan MacKay-Lyons looks almost impenetrable due to the homogeneity of the galvanized corrugated aluminum facade. The interior is done in warm materials, such as wood and ceramic. The huge windows help bring the outside in.

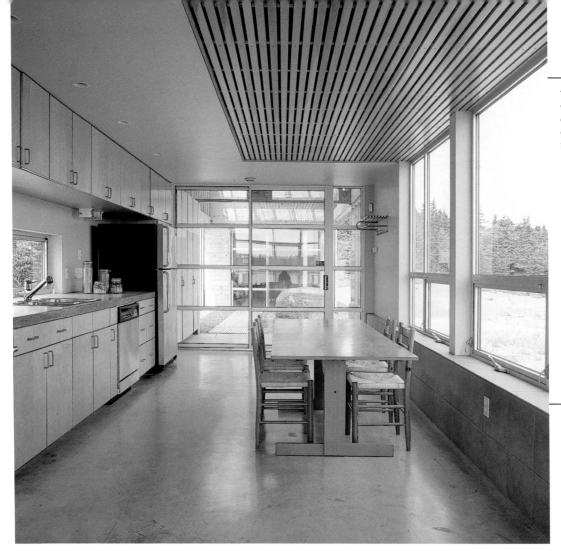

The kitchen floor is polished and waxed cement. The same material covers the lower parts of the concrete facade, affording continuity to the different levels.

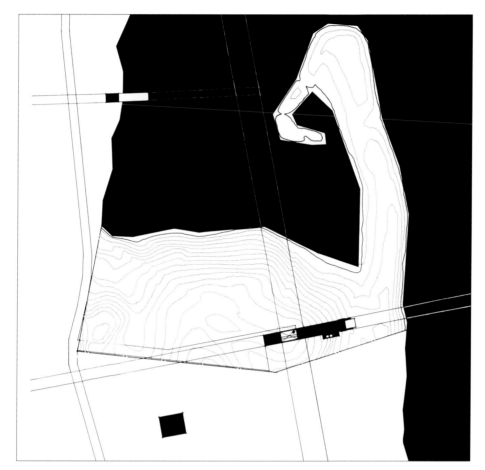

Site plan

N

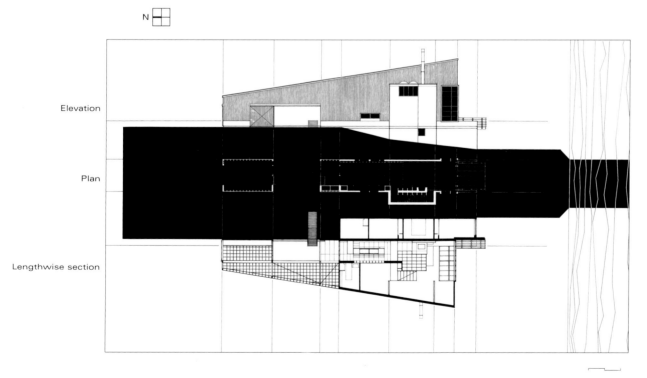

Elevation

Plan

Lengthwise section

0 1 2

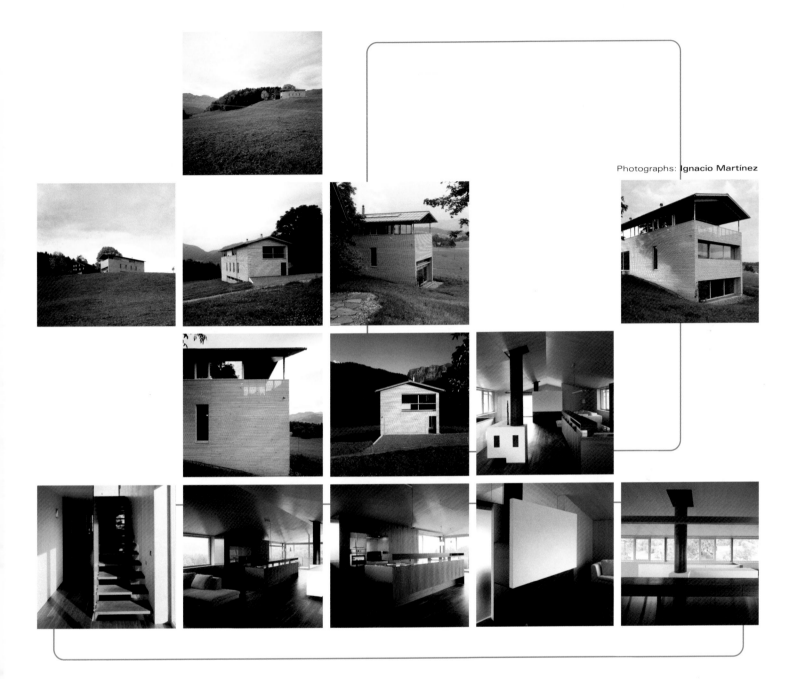

Photographs: Ignacio Martínez

Innfeld House

Dietrich + Untertrifaller Architekten

Collaborators: **Marina Hämmerle** Construction date: **1999** Location: **Schwarzenberger, Austria** Area: **3700 sq. feet**

The Innfeld House sits on the edge of a high plateau on the outskirts of the small Austrian town of Schwarzenberger. It seems to have landed there randomly, like the little shacks for drying grass that dot the nearby hills. No garden was planned, so the cultivated land comes right up to the building's foundation.

The nearby older house, typical of the region, emphasizes the modernity of this project by architects Helmut Dietrich and Much Untertrifaller, with its restrained lines, bereft of all ornamentation, which nevertheless harmonizes with the landscape and local architecture.

From the outset, the design process was influenced by the project's location. The designers wanted to make the most of the views of the surrounding valleys and the forests. So they planned a house whose upper level is almost transparent, with windows covering two thirds of the façade, and a large balcony, which is covered by the gabled roof.

At the rear of the house, facing northeast, three walls protect the private areas from the wind and cold. Just one sliding window and the access door break the thermal inertia of these solid walls.

The outer walls are covered with larch siding. The narrowness of the wooden strips and the fact that they come right to the corners of the building change the perception of the walls, giving the impression of a continuous flat surface, light and transpirable, concealing the bearing structure.

The traditional layout of household functions is reversed to ensure that the common areas enjoy the best views of the landscape. The bedrooms, on the ground floor, also have windows, but they are smaller and don't enjoy the same views.

Inside, the dark walnut floors contrast with the white walls and pale yellow of the pine woodwork. This heterogeneous combination of materials creates a warm, comfortable atmosphere conducive to relaxation and enjoyment of the scenery.

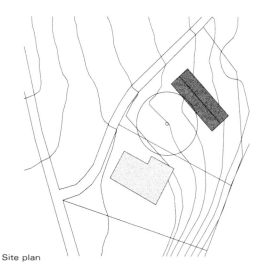

Site plan

Throughout the project, the structural skeleton is concealed: the gabled roof is supported by the walls at the rear of the house and by slender posts on the balcony, so it seems to be magically suspended above the domestic spaces.

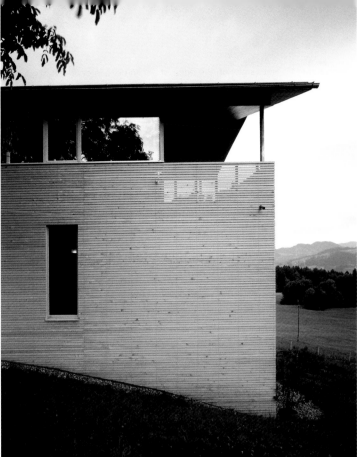

The placement of the lower-ground floor ensures that no room is without light. This level houses the utility rooms, the laundry room, and a storage area, and insulates the rest of the house from humidity.

The balcony, with exceptional views of the charming Voralberg area, has wood flooring. The rails are an extension of the outer walls, supported on slender posts anchored to the structure.

The living room, kitchen, and dining room occupy a single continuous space, which is dominated by the view of the scenery outside. Thanks to the enormous windows, the domestic spaces are flooded with natural light all day long. The kitchen furnishings were designed specifically for the project.

1. Laundry room
2. Bedrooms
3. Bathrooms
4. Master bedroom
5. Living room
6. Kitchen
7. Dining room
8. Balcony

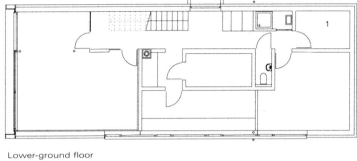

Lower-ground floor

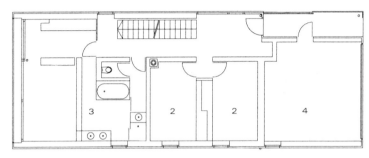

Ground floor

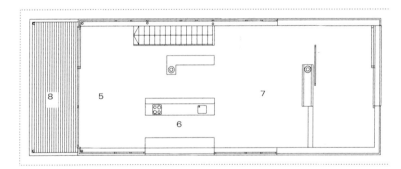

Second floor

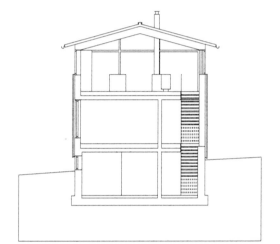

Cross Section

N

0   1   2

To contrast with the dark tones of the walnut flooring, most of the vertical surfaces are white or made of translucent glass, which allows light to enter without sacrificing privacy.

Photographs: **Philippe Ruault**

Marmonier Villa

Rudy Ricciotti

Construction date: **1999** Location: **La Garde, France** Area: **2680 sq. feet**

1. Terrace
2. Swimming pool
3. Addition

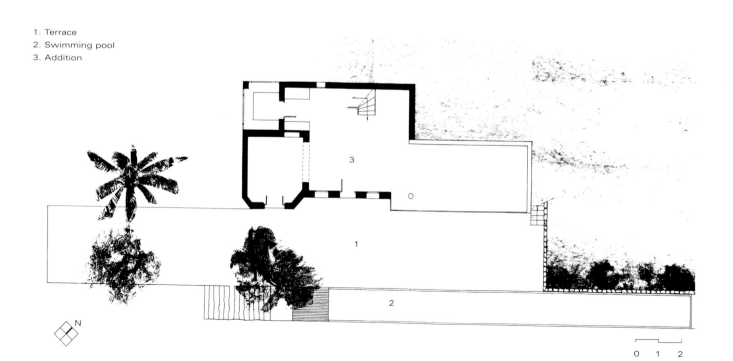

N

0 1 2

This project by Rudy Ricciotti, a famous architect who was born in Algiers and trained in France, consisted of remodeling and expanding a 1930's villa. He wanted to open the house up to the adjacent forest and enhance the views of the distant Mediterranean.

The lush plant life that surrounds the house and the moderate climate gave him a perfect opportunity to build a terrace with swimming pool. The pronounced slope of the land made it necessary to place both elements on a surface that projects above the landscape. To avoid having to use railings that would mar the views of the countryside, the swimming pool was placed on the edge of the platform. A net was installed below the retaining wall in case of falls.

A 176 sq. feet room leading to the terrace was added to the original building. To emphasize the relationship with the outdoors, the exterior wall is all glass, and there is no trim; the glass panels are joined to each other and to the floor with clear silicone. The roof is a large exposed concrete box that contains earth in which to plant shrubs. This dual function requires certain specific construction details, such as drainage for excess water, which is channeled off through tiny spouts. Supported by the exterior wall, the roof seems to float above the room.

Inside, the floor is wood and the walls are stucco. The simplicity of the lines contrasts with the materials of the old house: ceramic tile, painted textured stone, and wooden shutters. The furniture chosen for the new space, designed by the architect, emphasizes these contrasts.

The swimming pool, 23 m. long and 1.8 m. wide, was placed at the edge of the terrace to avoid having to use railings that would mar the views of the olive grove and cork oaks.

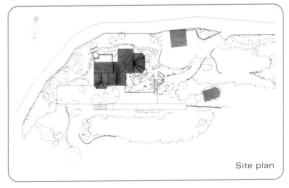

Site plan

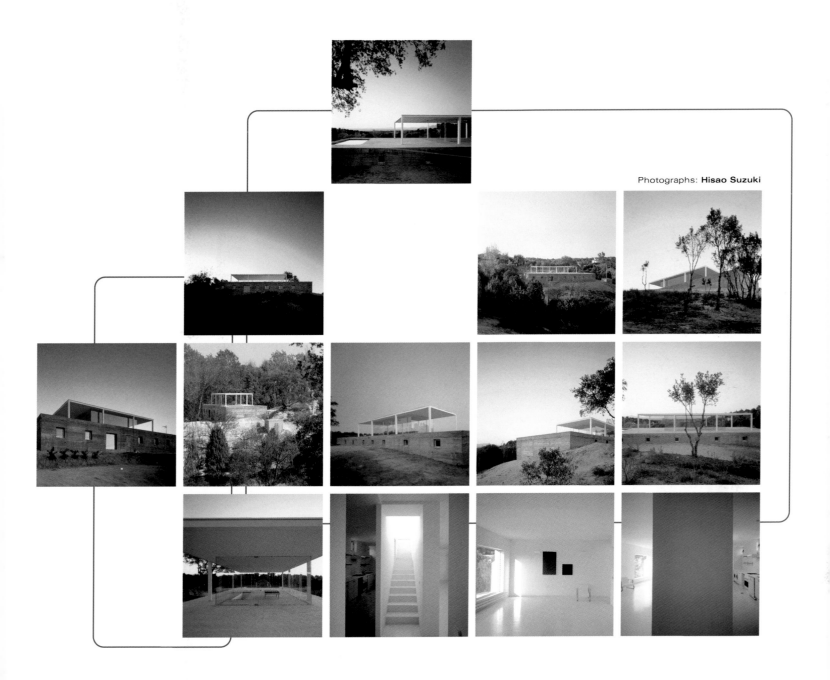

Photographs: **Hisao Suzuki**

De Blas House

Alberto Campo Baeza

Collaborators: **Raúl del Valle González** and **M.ª Concepción Pérez Gutiérrez**

Construction date: **2000** Location: **Sevilla la Nueva, Spain** Area: **2645 sq. feet**

The De Blas house is a brilliant piece of architecture, an ordered response to everyday needs and, above all, a tribute to the place where it is located. The building, which consists of a glass structure on top of a concrete block, sits on the crest of a hill southeast of Madrid, and looks north toward splendid mountains.

The concrete structure is anchored to the ground and appears solid and unyielding. In addition to providing space for the domestic functions, it serves as a vantage point from which to take in the beauty of the landscape. The functional organization is clear and simple: the bedrooms, living room, and dining room are in the front of the house, facing north, and the service area, bathrooms, and traffic areas are in the rear.

The rooms on this floor embrace nature in two different ways: on the northern side, the square windows frame exquisite views, and on the southern side, the light and sky filter through tiny openings in the uppermost part of the wall.

The glass structure, resting atop the platform, is a vantage point that is accessed from the house proper. The scenery pours in on every side. Since the walls are glass and there is no woodwork, they become ethereal, intangible boundaries between the indoors and outdoors.

The roof, a sheet of white-painted steel, tops the belvedere. The supporting structure consists of eight double columns with a U-shaped section. The entire unit looks like a large transparent table with a white surface and trim, in contrast to the concrete platform.

The composition of the materials, the thorough attention to architectural detail, the suggestive use of light, and the variety of sensations it engenders, make the De Blas house both innovative and enduring. The architect who collaborated on this project, Raúl del Valle González, points out the timelessness of Campo Baeza's work: "Beyond the ages, fashions, and styles, beyond time itself, he builds a Greek temple on the eve of the twenty-first century, and transforms the closed, dark, and secret cell of the gods into a transparent, luminous enclosure for man's enjoyment."

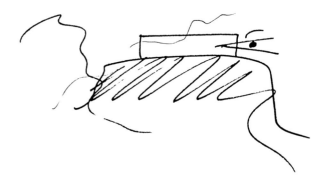

At one end of the concrete platform is a small swimming pool which, besides cooling the air in summer, is the source of countless reflections that play over the exterior walls and roof.

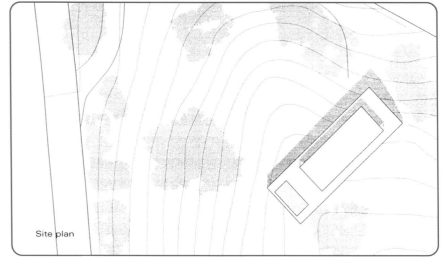

Site plan

Alberto Campo Baeza's sketches show the process of determining how to anchor the building on the land: the slope of the ground becomes a refuge on top of which the vantage point is constructed.

Unlike the belevedere, the lower level is a solid unit. The northern façade has large square openings for panoramic views, while the south-facing exterior wall is dotted by just a few small windows near the top.

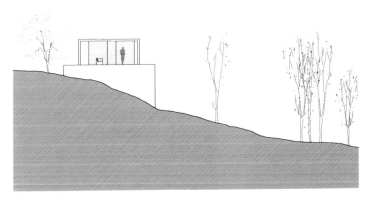

Western elevation

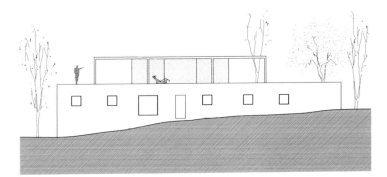

Cross-section

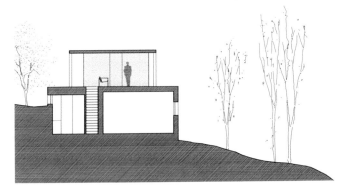

Northern elevation

0 1 2

1. Kitchen
2. Dining room
3. Living room
4. Bedrooms
5. Bathrooms
6. Swimming pool

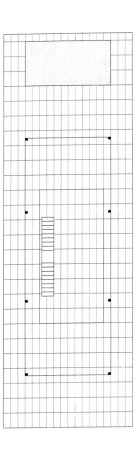

Second floor

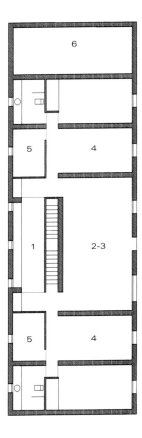

Ground floor

0 1 2

Photographs: **Undine Pröhl**

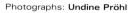

House and Art Gallery

Kennedy & Violich Architecture

Construction date: **1998**   Location: **Western Massachussets, USA**   Area: **6260 sq. feet**

This project by architects Kennedy and Violich incorporates an art gallery into an existing house. Their task included exterior landscape design to make it possible to exhibit works of art near the adjoining woods. The hybrid renovation plan included a dance studio, an office boasting the latest in telecommunications technology, an indoor swimming pool, a gallery of modern and contemporary art, two outdoor patios, and a sculpture garden.

The building had to fulfill all these varied functions in a single continuous space with abundant wall surfaces for hanging large paintings, works by Warhol, Oldenburg, and Christo, as well as small paintings and engravings. Other requirements included permitting views of the woods and allowing natural light to enter the art gallery while preventing the sun's rays from damaging the artwork.

The designers created a continuous series of six roof levels that join the existing building to the extension, which is organized around a 14-meter long swimming pool. Above it is a skylight that reflects the light from the west and directs it to the exhibit area. At night, this well of light acts like a vacuum where the light from the ceiling bulbs is reflected and creates a serene, constant environment.

For an orderly distribution of the utility systems, special cable housings were placed in the walls. Thin sheets of plywood were joined together and shaped into vertical partitions. So, the walls serve as exhibit space, miniature electrical infrastructures, and systems that support the whole.

The loft in which the study is located has a plywood floor which houses the telecommunications cabling and slopes to become an access ramp and accommodate shelving.

This house redefines the arrangement of household, leisure, and work space, and offers a setting for art which is a clear alternative to institutionalized museums and galleries. The project enriches the typical residential plans with new experiences, and inspires the clients to enjoy their works of art while they work or take care of personal business.

The swimming pool starts in the center of the gallery and extends to the ends of the building, to terminate in the projection overlooking the sculpture patio. The socle is reinforced concrete. The sides are covered with stone from the entry level on up.

The swimming pool is framed by a system of light ironwork that has been painted black. The ceiling of this small area is made of aluminum sheets, which reflect the light from the enormous windows onto the water.

The study floor is part of a plywood surface that starts with the stairs, which go up to the loft and turn to pass above the swimming pool. It also forms shelving with state-of-the-art technology.

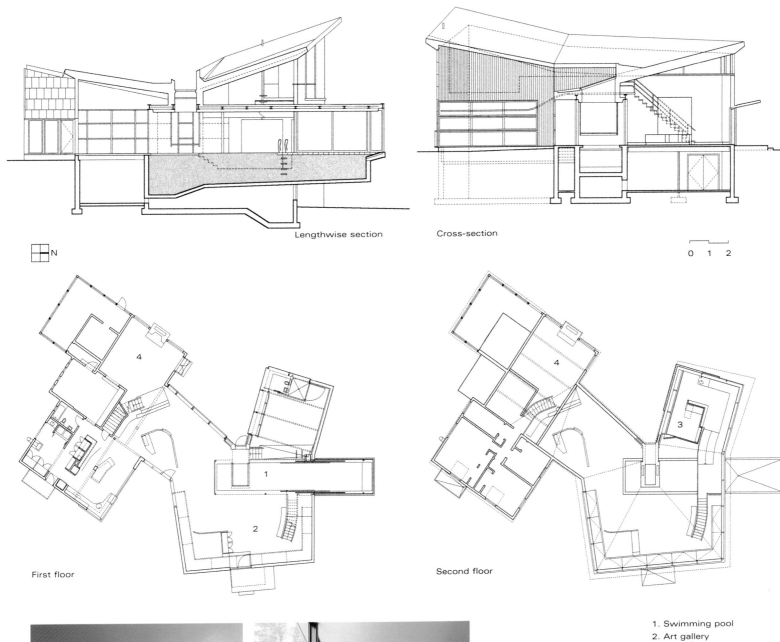

Lengthwise section

Cross-section

N

0 1 2

First floor

Second floor

1. Swimming pool
2. Art gallery
3. Study
4. Pre-existing house

Flexible wood surfaces that can be shaped and at the same time leave hollows for pulling cables serve as both a structural and finishing element.

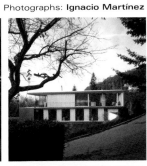

Photographs: **Ignacio Martínez**

Lingg House

Dietrich + Untertrifaller Architekten

Collaborators: **Marina Hämmerle** and **Albert Rüf**   Construction date: **2000**   Location: **Bregenz, Austria**   Area: **4300 sq. feet**

At night, the lights accentuate the compositional rhythm of the windows. The higher up you go, the more transparent are the exterior walls.

The staggering of the floors allows for the creation of intermediate spaces so the occupants can enjoy the outdoors without being exposed to inclement weather. For example, the second floor extends to protect the entrance from rain and the sun's rays. The upper level is set back, creating a space for a balcony.

The Lingg House is located on a hill on the outskirts of the city of Bregenz, with exceptional views of Lake Costanza. To the northeast, the structure is built into the ground to protect it from the coldest temperatures and increase the thermal inertia.

Due to construction complications and the additional expenses for moving earth, the house was set on a perpendicular with the slope. Only the part of the garden that faces south is actually at ground level. Naturally, at this point low reinforced concrete retaining walls break the continuity of the lawn.

The ground floor, which serves as a socle for the house, is also concrete and includes the entrance, the garage, and utility rooms. The second floor extends almost two meters out from the entrance, forming an overhang. This creates a comfortable, quiet intermediate space for greeting guests.

All the bedrooms are on the second floor. The children's rooms have direct access to the garden, and the parents' room enjoys views of the lake, thanks to the huge window in the western façade. To minimize traffic on this level, the stairs are positioned along one of the outer walls; they interfere with no domestic activity. On the third floor, the compartmentalization disappears and the living room, kitchen, and dining room occupy a single space, ending with the exterior balcony, which is covered by an extension of the roof. A narrow corridor connects the balcony with the higher ground.

The facades combine different materials: concrete, metal strips, and plywood, chosen for their functional versatility and colors that contrast with the surroundings.

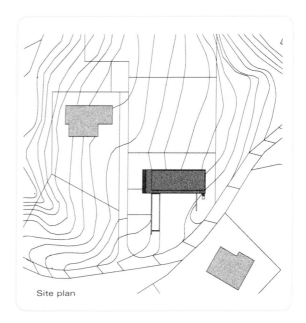

Site plan

Architects Dietrich and Untertrifaller gave priority to the placement of the many rooms with respect to the exterior. The strategic placement of the bedrooms and the common area means that all the spaces have large windows. In some places, translucent glass was used for the sake of privacy.

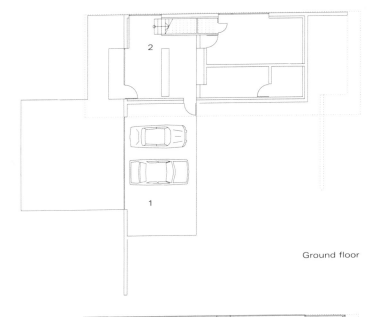

Ground floor

1. Garage
2. Entrance
3. Bedrooms
4. Lavatory
5. Bathroom
6. Master bedroom
7. Swimming pool
8. Fireplace
9. Living room
10. Balcony
11. Kitchen

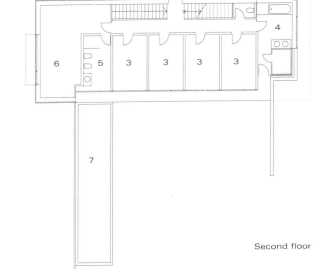

Second floor

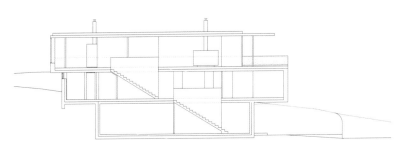

Lengthwise section

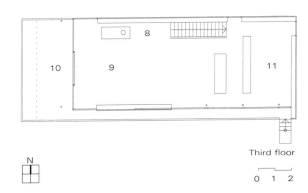

Third floor

N

0 1 2

Photographs: **Catherine Tighe**

McMackin Residence

Price Harrison

Collaborator: **Marilyn McMackin** Construction date: **1996** Location: **Nashville, Tenessee, USA** Area: **3495 sq. feet**

This single family home was designed to meet the clients' requirements: the project had to preserve the indigenous countryside and the building had to have a terrace from which the beautiful view could be savored. Price Harrison gives prominence to the outdoor areas, the terraces, swimming pool, and the porches, which act as a transition area between the residence and the natural world. To emphasize this relationship and enhance the views, the surrounding walls were built very low to the ground.

Platforms connected by small sets of stairs even out the slight irregularities of the terrain.

The swimming pool occupies one corner of the grouping and is protected by low walls that ensure privacy without blocking the view.

A patio at the entrance divides the house into two sections: one consists of two floors containing the common areas, the guest room, and a study, while the other, just one story high, contains the master bedroom and the garage.

The walls of the various rooms reflect their functions: the foyer, living room, and dining room are almost entirely enclosed by glass, while the more intimate spaces, such as the bedrooms and bathrooms, have just one small, elongated window. The alternating of transparent and opaque walls, and the placement of the openings, result in an aesthetically interesting arrangement which meets the users' needs.

The choice of materials took the setting into consideration, paying tribute to the natural beauty of the area while defining the minimalist architectural shapes of the two sections. The facade was covered with a stucco/stone mixture which was left unpainted to let its natural gray tones show through. The roof and drain holes are brass; the terraces, concrete; and the tops of the walls are limestone. The interior was done in warm materials, with light wood for the floor, plaster on the walls, and mahogany woodwork.

The furniture was carefully chosen by the owner, who worked closely with the architect on planning the interiors. The light tones create a warm, bright atmosphere.

Sometimes, the only thing separating the indoors from mother nature is glass. Intermediate spaces, such as terraces, were avoided to give the users a direct view of the surroundings.

The kitchen contains one piece of furniture without wood or stainless steel, facing a row of cupboards. The strategic placement of a window between the two rows of cupboards allows users to enjoy the scenery while washing dishes.

The small windows in the staircase and private rooms provide continuous illumination. When the sun is in the right place, bright shafts of light shine directly into corners or on objects.

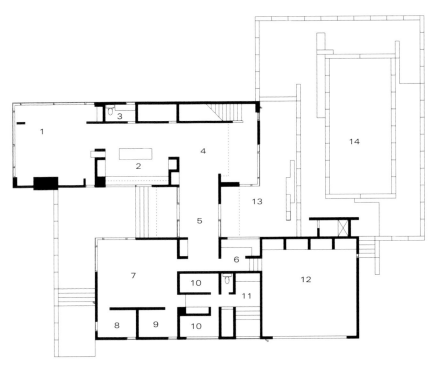

Ground floor

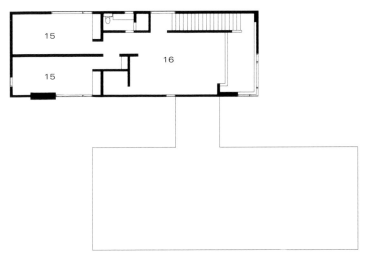

Second floor

 N

0 1 2

1. Living room
2. Kitchen
3. Lavatory
4. Dining room
5. Entrance
6. Laundry room
7. Master bedroom
8. Office
9. Gym
10. Closets
11. Bathroom
12. Garage
13. Fountain
14. Swimming pool
15. Bedrooms
16. Study

Photographs: **Eugeni Pons**

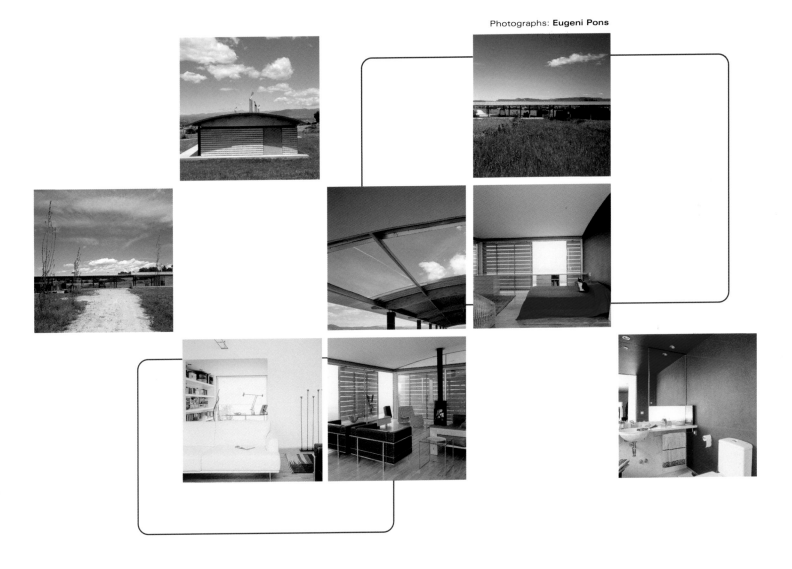

Piu House

Tonet Sunyer

Collaborator: **Eduardo Doce** Construction date: **1997** Location: **Vic, Spain** Area: **2365 sq. feet**

The Piu house project started off with a very low budget, so one of the priorities was to create a structure that the clients could add to as the opportunity arose. The site is located on the highway between Vic and Tavernoles, in the province of Barcelona. The building was placed far back on the lot, in a straight line, supported on three platforms that adjust for the unevenness of the land. The lowest level includes five stables for horses, while the living quarters were installed on the highest part of the lot.

The road leading to the house crosses the plot lengthwise, avoiding the slope, and divides the lot into two areas at different elevations: one for the horses, and the other, for the domestic areas, which was landscaped. In the future, a wall will enclose the swimming pool, the parking area, and the guest quarters, which are on the middle platform.

The residence, stables, and garage are sheltered by a pergola that unifies the grouping horizontally and provides shade along the entire length of the structure. These small terraces create an intermediate space between the interior and the outdoors.

The swimming pool is perpendicular to the house, parallel to the access road. Rows of black poplars were planted in front of the house.

The plan consists of two linear strips: on the northern side are the service areas, such as the kitchen and bathrooms; and on the southern side, the living room, dining room, and bedrooms. The master bedroom is located at one end and has an adjoining bathroom and ample dressing room.

The model of the Piu house clearly shows the placement of the grouping: the stables for the horses, the guest area, and the residence are placed on three different platforms. The pergola, which is the same height throughout, unites and harmonizes all the elements.

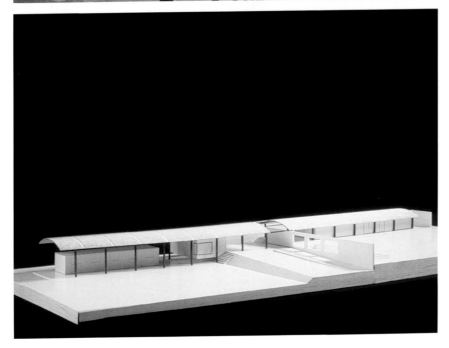

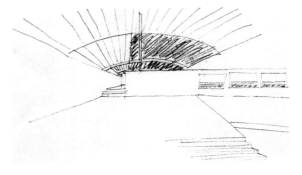

The master bedroom is located at one end and enjoys views in two directions. To filter the light and preserve the intimacy of the interior, the windows were covered with wooden slats.

The living room is at the other end of the residence, adjoining a porch that leads to the swimming pool. This connection with the exterior heightens the feeling of spaciousness in the common areas.

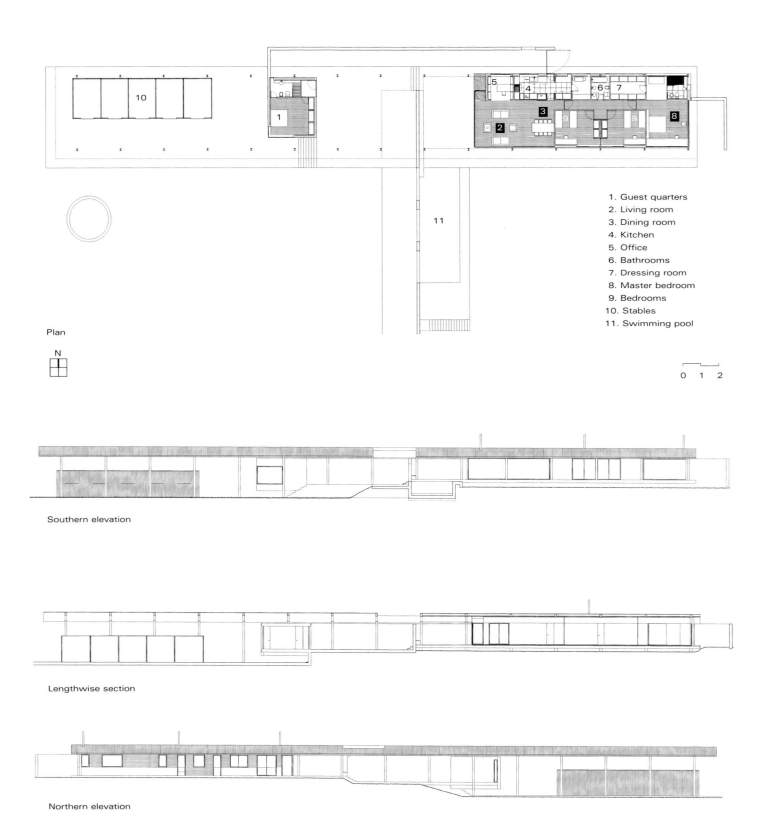

Plan

N

0 1 2

1. Guest quarters
2. Living room
3. Dining room
4. Kitchen
5. Office
6. Bathrooms
7. Dressing room
8. Master bedroom
9. Bedrooms
10. Stables
11. Swimming pool

Southern elevation

Lengthwise section

Northern elevation

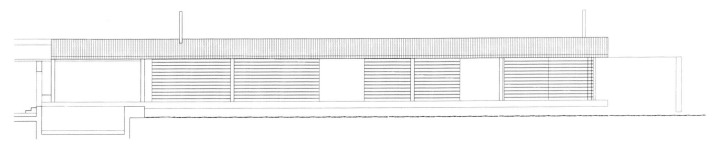

Southern elevation of the residence

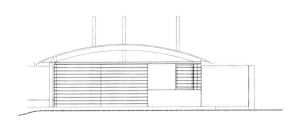

Eastern elevation of the residence

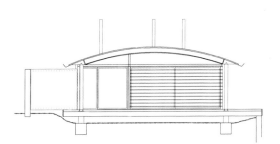

Western elevation of the residence

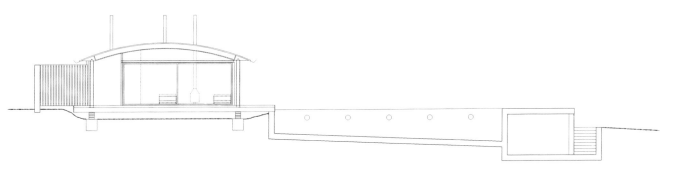

Cross-section of the swimming pool

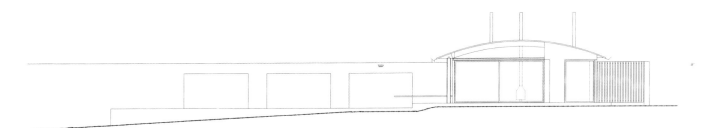

Cross-section of the living room

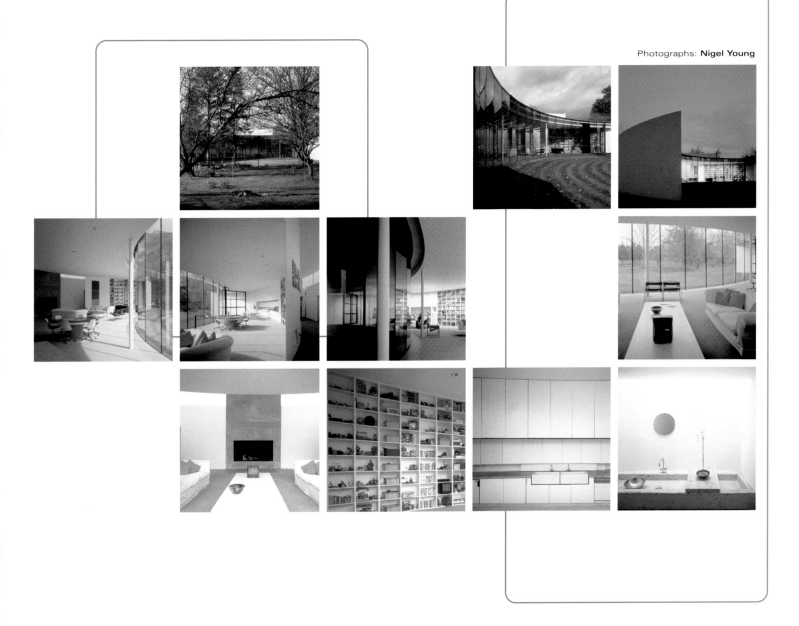

Photographs: **Nigel Young**

Crescent House

Ken Shuttlerworth

Collaborators: **Ove Arup & Partners (structures)**   Construction date: **1998**   Location: **Wiltshire, United Kingdom**   Area: **3225 sq. feet**

To the southeast, the Crescent House opens onto a splendid garden. The large glass wall blurs the distinction between indoors and outdoors. At the rear of the house, light filters through high windows, making the private rooms more intimate and peaceful.

Before beginning the plan for their home, Ken and Seana Shuttleworth established the basic idea of what it should be: a spacious, bright place that was both functional and in harmony with the setting. The result is a modest, austere building that reflects the many contrasts of the site and its historical context.

The land is in the heart of Wiltshire, one of the most beautiful rural areas in England. The dilapidated existing buildings were demolished. To make the most of the views, the house was placed in the northwestern corner of the lot. Thus, car traffic was reduced and most of the land could remain undeveloped.

The site is accessed through a gate hidden among the trees. A large curved wall greets the visitor and guides him toward the entrance while directing his gaze to the magnificent garden. At the end of the wall, the entire residence comes into view: two half moons connected by a two-story gallery, at the end of which is the entrance.

All the private spaces are located in the semicircular structure facing northwest, which is opaque to provide protection from the wind and ensure privacy. The bedrooms, bathrooms, and dressing rooms are small, peaceful rooms provided with light from above.

The semicircle facing southeast has views of the garden, thanks to an all-glass wall. The dining room, kitchen, and living room are in a single continuous space with 11-foot ceilings, flooded with natural light and in direct contact with the surrounding natural environment.

All the traffic areas are concentrated in the intermediate gallery, which provides a transition between the common area and private spaces. The narrowest part of this corridor contains an enormous fireplace whose chimney rises above the building and can be seen from a distance.

From the outset, the design was influenced by an intense ecological awareness. More than a thousand trees were planted. Those closest to the building protect it from the wind, provide shade in the summer, and let the sunlight pass through in the winter. Another means of saving energy was the installation of thermal insulation in the walls and ceiling.

In addition, an area has been set aside for solar plates and receptacles for collecting rainwater, but these have not yet been put to use.

In keeping with local tradition, the house was painted entirely in white. The effect is one of abundant luminosity that changes with the curvature of the walls or the appearance of windows, molding the environment to reflect the time of day and season of the year.

The atmosphere in the domestic areas changes with the seasons. On the one hand, the light leaves the mark of every season, and on the other, the decorative elements, such as cushions and vases, change in contrast with the climate: red for winter, yellow for spring, blue for summer, and green for autumn.

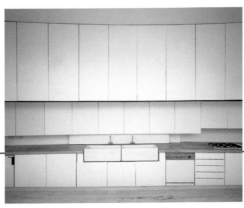

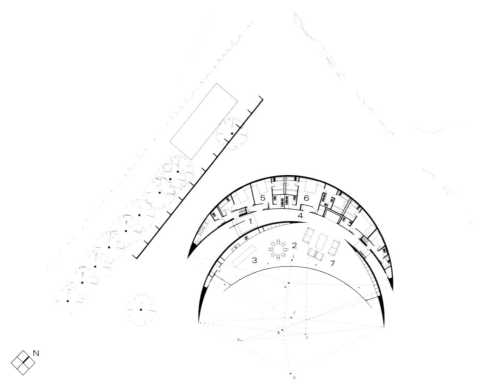

1. Entrance
2. Dining room
3. Kitchen
4. Dining room
5. Bedrooms
6. Master bedroom
7. Living room

N

0 1 2

Site plan

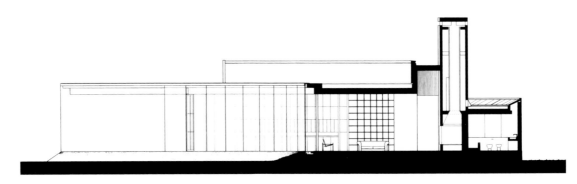

Lengthwise section

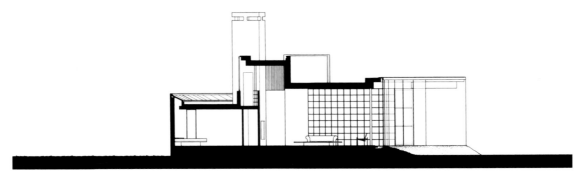

Cross-section

0 1 2

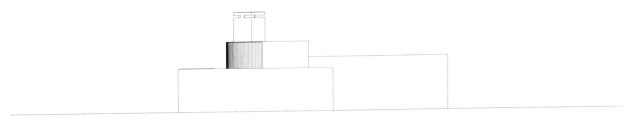

Northeastern elevation

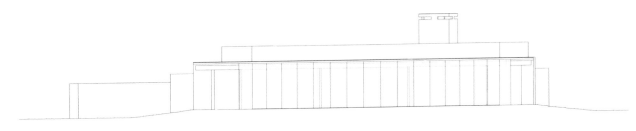

Southeastern elevation

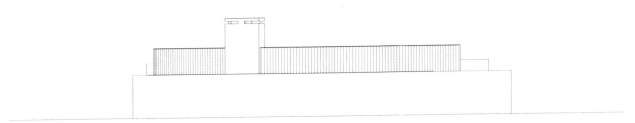

Northwestern elevation

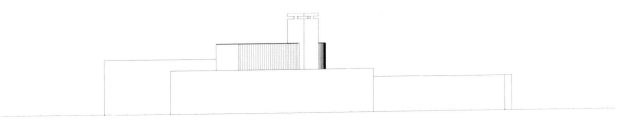

Southwestern elevation

0 1 2

A profound ecological awareness governed the entire design process. No trees were cut down, and more than a thousand were planted to establish an energy-saving microclimate.
An area for solar plates and rainwater storage was provided.

Erlandson Villa

Per Friberg Arkitektbyrå

Construction date: **1999** Location: **Ljunghusen, Sweden** Area: **2470 sq. feet**

The Erlandson villa sits in a forest clearing. The unique location of the plot determined the architects' and clients' requirements. The surrounding natural setting could not be altered for the house. Also, the domestic spaces had to take advantage of the natural light offered by the absence of trees in the immediate vicinity of the structure.

The house was built on a wooden platform to protect it from the damp Nordic climate. This strategy makes almost no difference in the overall appearance, other than enhancing the sense of lightness. The ethereal quality of the facades and interior partitions emphasizes this effect.

The layout is fairly conventional: the common rooms are on the first floor and the private rooms are on the upper floor, which also includes a generous balcony that offers views of the surrounding area. The hall and stairs were placed on the north side to avoid blocking the warm light entering from the south.

The predominant building material is wood, in deference to the concepts of ecology and comfort on which the design process was based. The framework consists of an orthogonal system of beams and posts that support the different parts of the building. The exterior walls are supported by vertical wooden uprights that also form the window frames. The construction details were carefully designed and remain visible to enhance the house's bright, solid appearance. This is especially apparent in the junctures of the structural elements or the eaves boards.

The house and terraces sit on a platform, supported by posts, a few centimeters above the ground.

Site plan

The balconies and terraces surrounding the Erlandson villa are made of wooden strips with a few millimeters of space between them to let the daylight shine through and give the building a light, ethereal look.

The interior and exterior walls are made entirely of wood. The living room has abundant glass for natural light and views of the garden. The furniture includes specially-designed pieces.

1 Kitchen
2 Dining room
3 Living room
4 Master bedroom
5 Bedrooms
6 Terrace
7 Bathroom

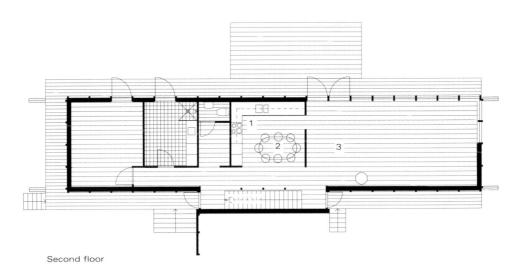

Second floor

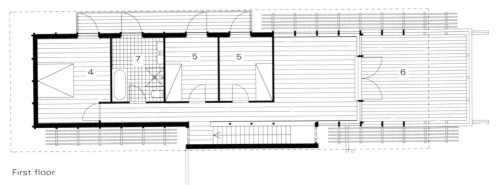

First floor

N

0 1 2

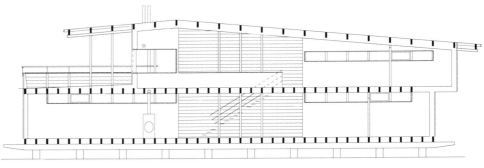

Section

The designers decided to place the stairs that connect the two floors alongside the rectangular residence. They do not take up space that could be otherwise used or interfere with household activities.

Photographer: **A.T. Neubau**

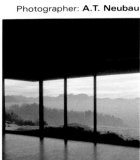

Häfenberg House

Gerold Wiederin

Construction date: **1999**　Location: **Dornbirn, Austria**　Area: **2850 sq. feet**

The house sits on a hill with magnificent views of Dornbirn, in the Austrian region of Vorarlberg, known for the quantity and quality of its architectural projects. To the northwest is a vast meadow, and to the south is a house belonging to the owner's parents. The residence and garage form a grouping about as large as the existing house. Many local farms have grown similarly over the years, adding buildings as the need arose.

To take advantage of the views and natural light, Gerold Wiederin placed the new house at the edge of the incline.

The two floors are staggered, creating a balcony on the eastern side. Both the eastern and western facades are all-glass, while the northern and southern sides are compact and closed despite the existence of two small windows. The brick walls are covered with a greenish-gray mineral mixture that emphasizes the project's solidity. The pigments produce reflections that play over the house, giving it an iridescence when the sun's rays hit it.

The landscaped roof and its unique triangular shape are visible from the street.

The lower floor, comprised of open, continuous spaces, is organized around a wooden core that houses the installations and means of access. The kitchen, built into this space, faces north. Strategically placed sliding doors separate the rooms. Large glass doors open onto the terraces, helping to bring the outdoors in. The polished concrete floor that covers the entire level emphasizes the relationship between both spaces.

The upper level, which is private and intimate, boasts a wide corridor that runs north-to-south and will be converted into a library. Its windows provide a whole new set of views that change the atmosphere of the residence. The flooring, made of small pieces of wood, gives this level a warm, comfortable feeling.

The exterior spaces await the intervention of landscape architects Kienast & Vogt, who will add the finishing touches to the site and shape concise, definitive vistas with their placement of trees and shrubs.

The Häfenberg house is a fine example of Vorarlberg's flourishing architecture. Gerold Wiederin takes his place alongside such greats as Baumschlager & Eberle or Diertich & Untertrifaller, having participated in the creation of an architectural paradise in this Austrian region.

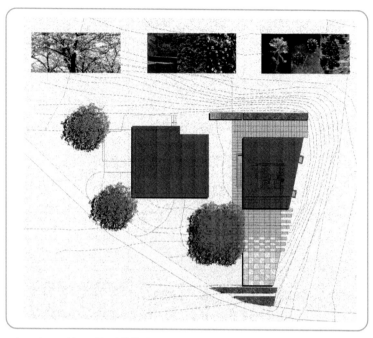

Austrian architect Gerold Wiederin's work is parallel to the existing building. The intent was to evoke the farm buildings, such as stables and barns, that are commonly locally.

The warm interior finishes, such as wood and polished concrete, contrast with a cold, heavy exterior.

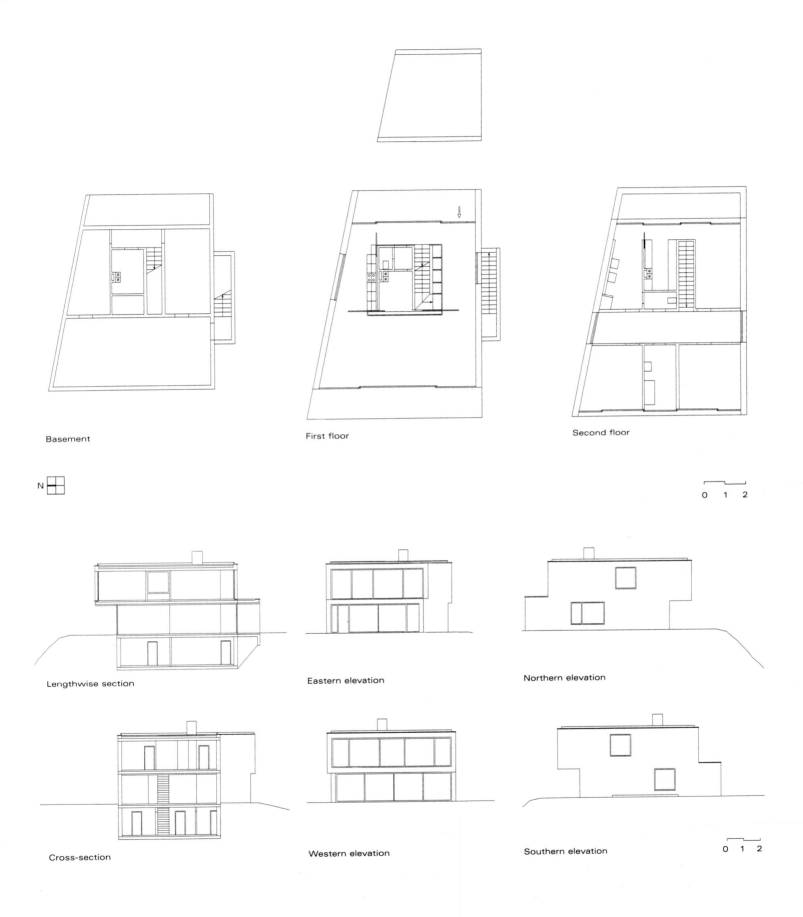

Basement

First floor

Second floor

N

0 1 2

Lengthwise section

Eastern elevation

Northern elevation

Cross-section

Western elevation

Southern elevation

0 1 2

Photographs: **Manos Meisen**

House in Italy

Döring Dahmen Joeressen Architekten

Collaborator: **Bernhard Korte**   Construction date: **2000**   Location: **Italy**   Area: **4300 sq. feet**

This rural home sits on top of a small hill in the Italian countryside. Due to its geographic location, the area is subject to earthquakes. The design took this risk consideration from the outset.

After a careful geological survey, the decision was made to build a reinforced concrete frame covered by brick walls to ensure rigidity, especially at the corners. This supporting system is arranged on a 5 meter grid which dictates the layout of the house.

The brick walls are covered by blocks of native tufa. The porosity of this volcanic material gives the solid, heavy structure an ethereal quality. Also, the thickness of the pieces, 25 cm., makes for 65 cm. walls, enabling the builder to install shutters. These are a real necessity in the sunny Mediterranean. Moreover, the thickness increases the building's thermal inertia, keeping it cool in summer and distributing the heat in the winter months.

The lower of the two levels contains an office and the rooms devoted to farming activities. The upper level, part of which, due to the slope of the land, is at ground level, contains the domestic spaces and a large terrace.

One of the goals of the design was to minimize the construction details to let the power of the structure shine through. Expert local artisans were engaged to help solve certain technical problems.

The severe shapes and profusion of right angles contrast with the curved shapes of the surrounding natural world and the organic structures Bernhard Korte placed in the garden. The two pines that were already on the site now coexist with beautifully-shaped olive trees, all personally selected by Korte.

Sketch of a nearby town

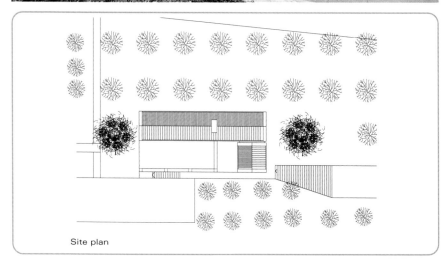

Site plan

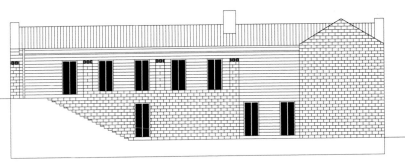

Southern elevation

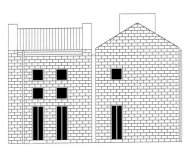

Eastern elevation

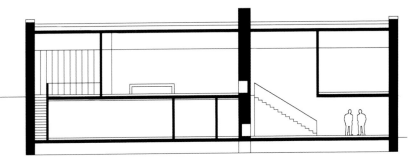

Lengthwise section

0 1 2

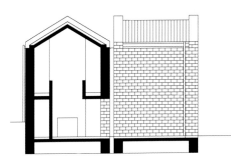

Cross-section

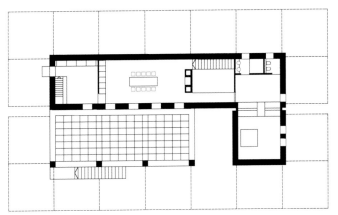

First floor

The interior spaces are just as unadorned as the exterior of the building. Right angles and simple geometric shapes dominate spaces illuminated through small openings in the solid walls.

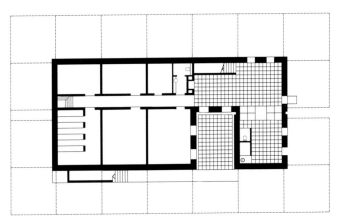

Second floor

N

0 1 2

Photographs: **Peter Kerze**

Hanson House

David Salmela

Construction date: **1997**   Location: **Northeastern Minnesota, USA**   Area: **1590 sq. feet**

At the clients' request, David Salmela surrounded the house with porches. Each is made of different quarterings of wooden planks.

The measurements had to be very precise, because the rough terrain meant that many of the elements would be in direct contact with the rock. Each of the stairs to the house is a different length, to fit the space between the building and the rock.

After their children left home, the Hansons decided to sell their house south of Minneapolis and rent an apartment downtown. This allowed them to buy a bucolic piece of land adjoining Quetico Provincial Park, renowned for its marvelous scenery.

When they were younger, the clients had camped near the shores of Lake Superior. So being able to buy a piece of land filled with fir trees and near a lake was the fulfillment of a long-held dream.

Lovers of modern architecture and admirers of the work of Alvar Aalto and Le Corbusier, the Hansons participated actively in the pre-design phase of the project, contributing ideas based on their needs and desires.

The location of the house, right on top of a rocky mass, was determined by US laws requiring buildings to be at least 50 meters back from the lakefront. The structure is built around a courtyard that includes the highest rock, making it the heart of the grouping.

The plan called for a dayroom and abundant sleeping space, inasmuch as the home will be a gathering place for the entire family during vacations. The living room, kitchen, and dining room face the lake and the central courtyard. For privacy, the bedrooms were placed in a loft and in the northern wing. This isolation does not keep the bedrooms from enjoying abundant natural light and views of the surroundings.

A small storehouse placed apart from the grouping is reminiscent of the old barns found on local farms.

A platform resting on concrete pillars supports the wooden beams and posts of the framework. The courtyard walls were inspired by Alvar Aalto's Muuratsalo house in Finland, but in this project the walls are strips of painted or varnished wood rather than brick.

The brilliance of this project lies in having taken the rocky mass, which at first was the main obstacle to construction, and made it the focal point of the grouping, around which all the rooms of the house are arranged. Moreover, the project combines the qualities of the old wooden cabins with modern layouts that take advantage of the views and natural light.

Although it sits amid the lush woods, the house, situated on the crest of a hill, is visible from various points.

The construction details demonstrate the architect's expertise with wood. The joinings of the framework and the facades, the window frames and the staircase, are magnificent examples of a good artisan's skill.

1 Entrance
2 Living room
3 Porch
4 Laundry room
5 Bathroom
6 Dressing room
7 Bedrooms
8 Loft
9 Offices
10 Storehouse

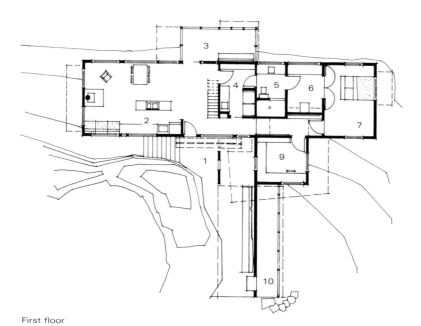

First floor

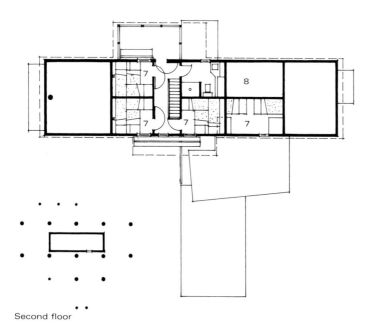

Second floor

N

0　1　2

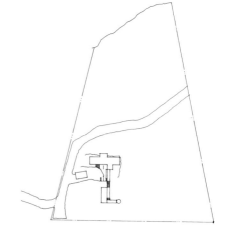

Site plan

Most of the furniture is built in. The closets, some sofas, and the many beds were made of wood, just for the project. This strategy unifies the grouping and provides comfort and convenience.

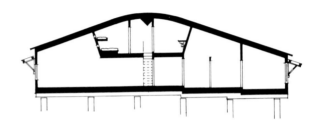

Section

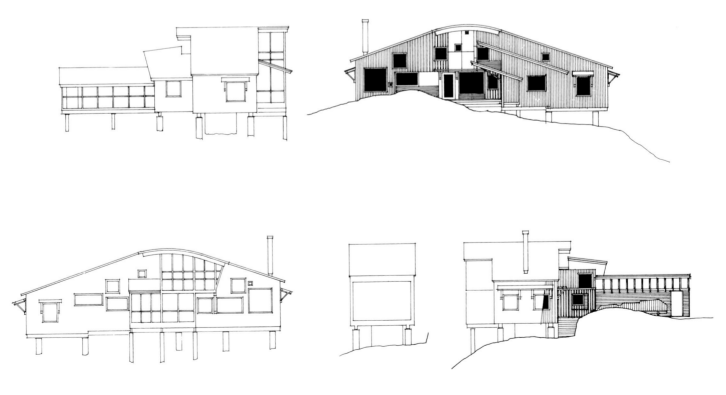

Elevations

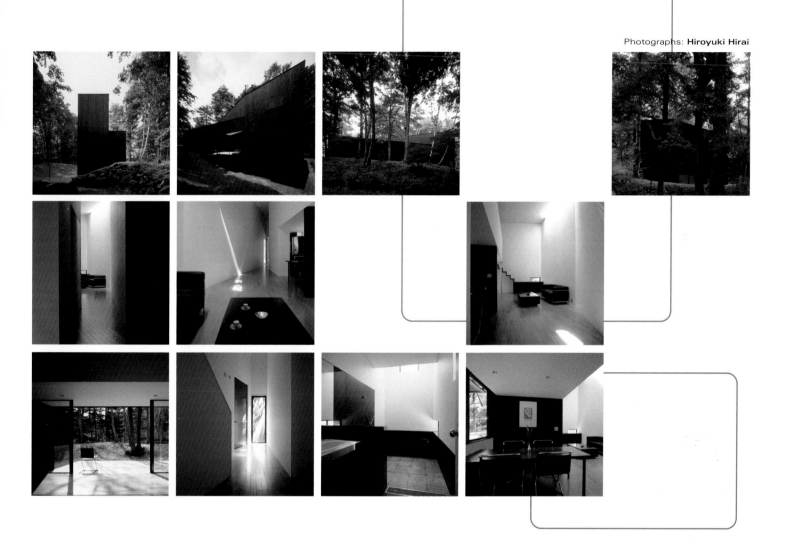

Photographs: **Hiroyuki Hirai**

House on Mount Fuji

Satoshi Okada

Collaborators: **Lisa Tomiyama** and **Eisuke Aida** Construction date: **2000** Location: **Narusawa Village, Japan** Area: **1480 sq. feet**

This house is located at the base of Mount Fuji, in an area of thick vegetation boasting many trees. The terrain is rugged due to its past volcanic activity: the lava solidified and left hillocks which, with the passage of time, were covered with grass and deciduous plants.

The plot is long, extending northeast-southwest, and is bounded by two roads. The peacefulness and isolation of the beech and birch forests is broken only by a nearby cabin.

For architect Satoshi Okada, this project was a poetic exercise. The Japanese respect for nature is evident throughout, from the choice of materials to the anchoring of the house on the ground. The building is like a monument, a structure that is solid but camouflaged amid the foliage, a "shadow in the forest," according to Okada.

The clients commissioned this small weekend home so they could enjoy the tranquility of the location with their guests. The building was situated in the northeastern corner of the lot, so as to take advantage of the abundant natural light and still remain private. A roof with multiple slopes is in harmony with the uneven terrain.

A large diagonal wall divides the house into two segments: a spacious area housing the common domestic functions, and another area for the bedrooms and bathrooms. At the entrance, a long, dark corridor widens to become an enormous gallery illuminated by light from above. This space contains a loft below which the kitchen and dining room were placed, with ceilings barely two meters high, in contrast to the five meter ceilings in the living room.

A small hall leads to the bedrooms, sheltered behind the wall. A gap in the upper part of the wall provides light for the residents in the private areas of the building.

Like the architectural forms, the materials chosen harmonize with the peaceful surroundings. So wood is used throughout. The façade is cedar stained black, and the floor is covered with oak parquet. For reasons of practicality, the bathroom and terrace floors are granite.

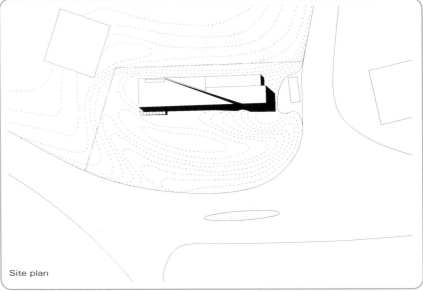

Site plan

The building is clearly outlined under the treetops and above the lava it attempts to emulate. The house is accessed by means of a short ramp that bridges the gap between the ground and the entrance, which are at two different levels.

At some points the façade appears to be an impregnable wall, but at others, the sections are differentiated and the arrangement of the interior domestic space is revealed.

The exterior walls are set back at certain points to shape terraces that afford views of the surroundings and provide an enclave for outdoor living. Overhangs provide protection from inclement weather.

There are few doors inside. Rooms are delimited by gaps in the walls and light entering from above.

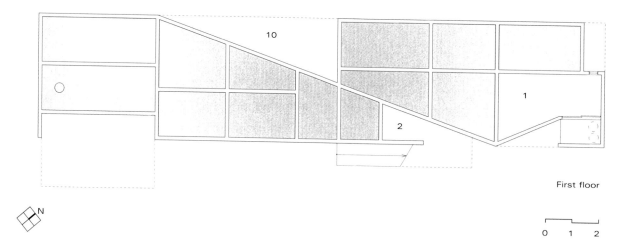

1. Storage area
2. Machine room

First floor

N

0   1   2

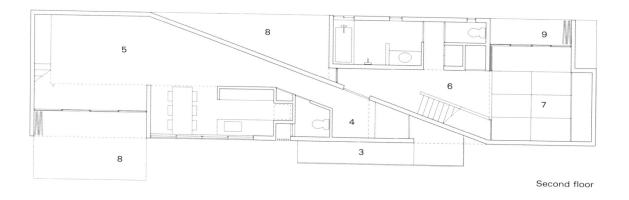

3. Ramp
4. Entrance
5. Living room
6. Hall
7. Tatami room
8. Terrace
9. Balcony
10. Patio

Second floor

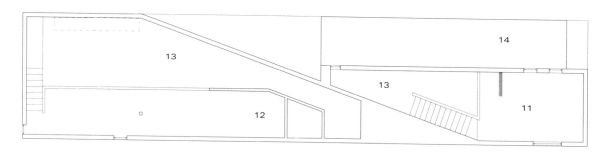

11. Bedroom
12. Loft
13. Empty space
14. Roof

Third floor

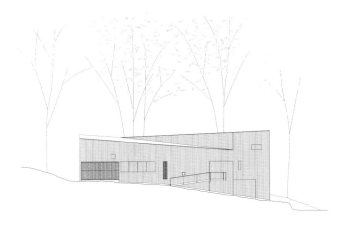

Southeast elevation

Southwest elevation

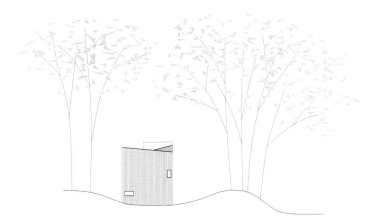

Northwest elevation

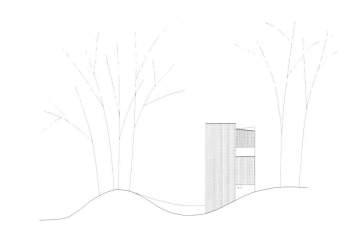

Northeast elevation

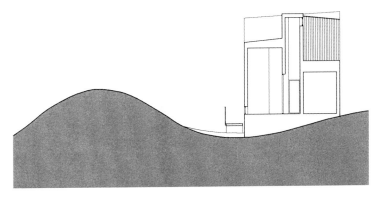

Cross-section

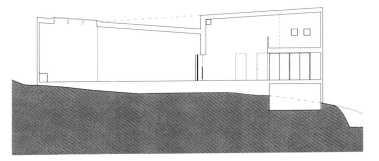

Lengthwise section

0 1 2

Photographs: **Fernando Cordero**

House in Celaya
Grupo LBC

Collaborators: **Guillermo Flores** and **Octavio Cardozo**   Construction date: **1996**   Location: **Celaya, Mexico**   Area: **3870 sq. feet**

The project by Grupo LBC (Alfonso López Baz and Javier Calleja Ariñol) consists of two elegant buildings resting on a hillock amid the landscaped plain of the San Rafael ranch outside the city of Celaya.

Since it is a horse ranch, much of its ten hectares is landscaped and divided into corrals where the horses are trained and rest. There are also outdoor showjumping rings, indoor rings, and stables for some thirty horses.

The residence overlooks the main showjumping ring, which is near an area thick with hundred-year-old trees. From a distance, the complex is a metaphor of white fences dividing the pastures and contrasting with the green hues of the landscaped areas.

The plan consists of two structures, simultaneously joined and separated by a mirror of water that has both practical and aesthetic functions. As it produces reflections it increases the humidity and the sensation of coolness in a dry climate where it is not unusual for the temperature to reach forty degrees centigrade. Above the water, wooden footbridges connect the two structures.

The structures are covered by vaulted ceilings. While high in the center, the rooms retain their domestic feel. The curvilinear shape of these ceilings, moreover, allows for uniform reflection of the natural light that enters through the facades.

The service rooms and fireplaces were set against the front and back walls, which have hardly any openings to the outside. The lateral walls have huge windows which face the showjumping rings.

Around the house are several terraces covered by canvas stretched over poles. These provide shade and views of the plain unhampered by glare.

The vaulted roof is completely smooth, with nothing to detract from enjoyment of its beauty. The lights and ventilation grilles were placed on the walls.

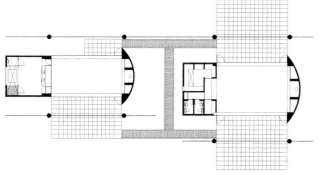

First floor

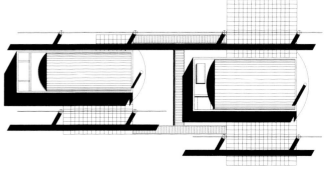

Plan of the roofs

N

0 1 2

The lengthwise windows in the living room were installed without woodwork so the views would be clear and direct. Access to this room is through a door in one of the corners.

Lengthwise section

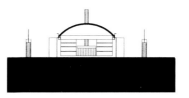

Cross-section

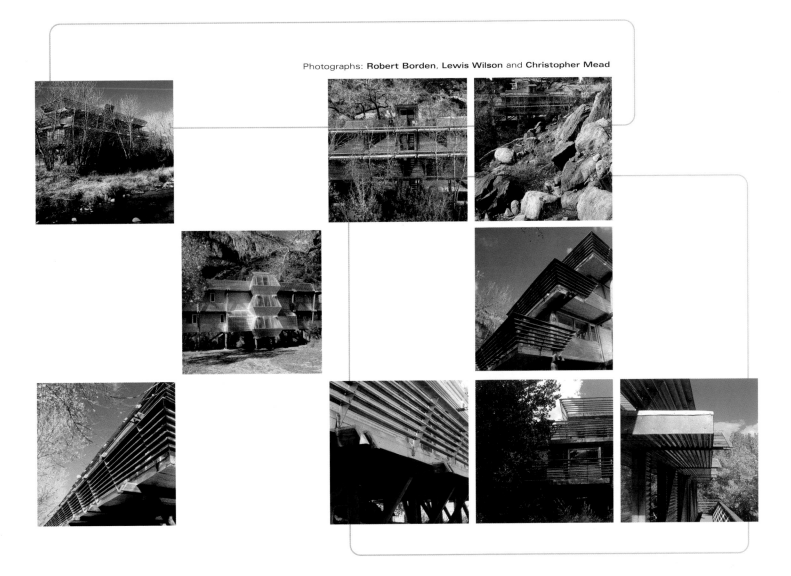

Photographs: **Robert Borden**, **Lewis Wilson** and **Christopher Mead**

Borden-Wiegner Residence

Bart Prince

Collaborator: **J. Kory Baker**   Construction date: **1998**   Location: **Jémez Springs, New Mexico, USA**   Area: **1800 sq. feet**

The Borden-Wiegner residence is the result of close collaboration between the owners, who contributed the concept and specific domestic requirements, and Bart Prince, who dazzled them with his talent, perfectly realizing all their desires.

For years, the clients had dreamed of leaving the hustle and bustle of Jémez Springs, New Mexico, and building a house in the country. They started by buying a charming lot on the banks of the Jémez River, with views of the tableland and scores of poplars. After living for some time in a trailer on the land, they hired Prince to design their dream house.

Because of the risk of flooding, the house was built on a platform supported by pine posts. Laminated wood beams support the framework. The house is symmetrical on both sides of a central staircase. Each floor has a balcony that almost completely surrounds it.

The lower floor of the residence contains the common areas (kitchen, living room, dining room, and office) and a guest room. The bedrooms are on the middle floor, and the loft boasts a spectacular balcony.

The uniqueness of the materials and construction details employed by Bart Prince complicated the search for a builder.

The outer walls were covered with corrugated metal siding, except, of course, for the window areas. The balcony railings are slender metal slats supported by uprights that provide a sense of continuity. In addition, the galvanized metal and glass staircase rises above the façade. The metal finish reflects the sunlight in myriad ways and gives the house a futuristic appearance.

The metal facades give the house a futuristic appearance. The neighbors have dubbed it "the spaceship." It is not surprising that the owners often see curiosity-seekers stopping on the road to marvel at this unique structure. To ensure that the house would blend with the landscape, Bart Prince decided to make it appear light: the posts on which it rests allow the vast expanse of the land to be seen. The spaces between the balconies also keep the views of the natural surroundings from being blocked.

The amount of floor space decreases gradually for functional reasons and to take advantage of the sun and the magnificent blue sky. Each level enjoys a generous balcony.

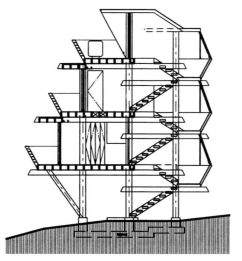

Cross-section

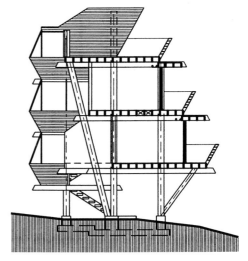

Cross-section

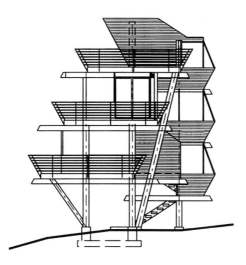

Southern elevation

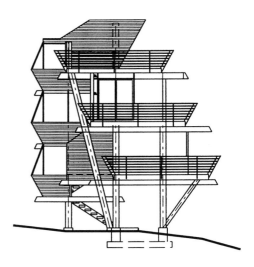

Northern elevation

0 1 2

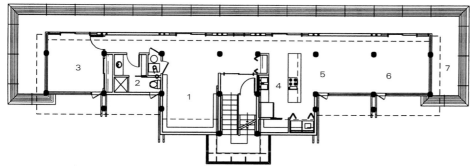

First floor

 N

1 Study
2 Bathroom
3 Guest room
4 Kitchen
5 Dining room
6 Living room
7 Balcony

0 1 2

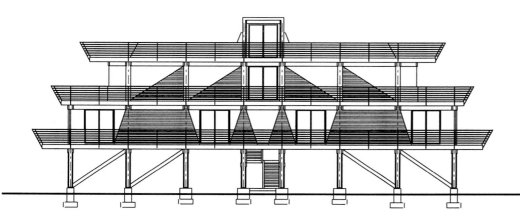

Western elevation

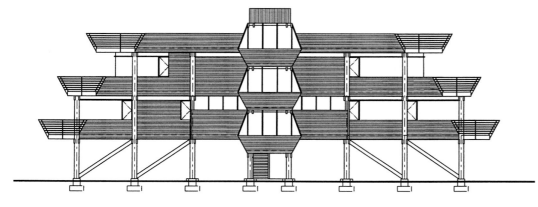

Eastern elevation

Bart Prince's unique, abstract works are not the result of esthetic whim, but reflect the needs of a society and a place. The Borden-Wiegener house is a real tribute to the mountains and deserts of the New Mexico landscape.

Photography: **Jan Erik Ejenstam** and **Erik Ståhl**

Arketorp Villa

Erik Ståhl

Collaborators: **Erik Persson** and **Rolf Almqvist**   Construction date: **2000**   Location **Jönköping, Sweden**   Area: **5100 sq. feet**

Architect Erik Ståhl always designs his projects to be timeless. His buildings are durable, thanks to the quality of the materials used, and classical, since he uses shapes that avoid fads or whims.

This Swedish architect bases his design strategy on the relationships between form and function, materials and textures, space and light. These parameters, appropriately incorporated into the specific setting of each project, result in structures that are lasting, functional, and esthetic.

The goal of this project was to preserve local historic and cultural values and create sensual, decorous architecture undisturbed by artifice or affectation.

The lot chosen for this single-family home is located in a rural area just 7 kilometers from the heart of the small city of Jönköping. The spectacular views of a forest of oak trees and nearby Lake Vättern make the spot truly unique.

Great care was taken to save the existing trees and keep the natural surroundings intact. No artificial garden was planned, other than arranging the plants on the patio at the entrance to resemble a Japanese garden, but adapted to Swedish culture and personal preferences.

The building is fully in tune with the architect's exquisite sensitivity to nature. Accordingly, he sought a close relationship between the interior and the outdoors, especially to enhance enjoyment of the landscape during the longed-for Swedish summer. One can savor views of the surrounding plant life from any point in the house.

The house is organized around a central corridor from which two small halls branch off. These connect all the rooms. This system of passages affords multiple connections and creates many meeting places, small vestibules in front of all the rooms, that enhance relationships among the residents.

The natural light and the choice of materials emphasize the concept of the project as a home surrounded by nature. Birch plywood is the predominant material for the walls and ceilings. In stark contrast, the door and window frames were painted dark brown. In the small bedrooms the floor is made of beechwood, and in the rest of the house, the flooring is ceramic glass.

Site plan.

Different surfaces around the house mark the transition between plant life and building. At some points, small wooden terraces were built. Gravel was spread in front of the private areas to discourage passers-by. Different levels are joined by sturdy stairs of exposed concrete.

The exterior is covered with pine. The wood was pressure treated to protect it from the ravages of climate and insects. The exterior window and door frames were painted dark brown.

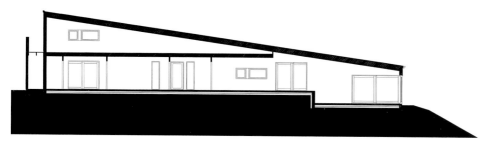

Lengthwise section

0　1　2

In keeping with Erik Ståhl's respect for nature, the main section of the building emulates the slope of the land. Despite the slope, the roof was waterproofed with a tar-based asphalt.

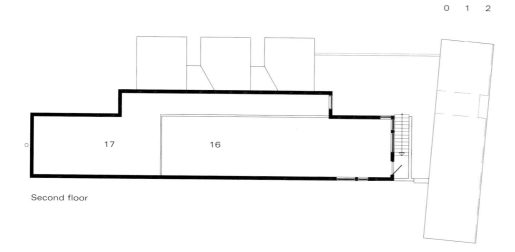

17　16

Second floor

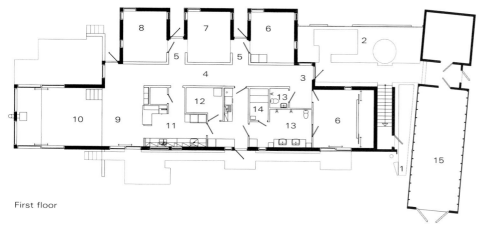

8　7　6

2

5　5

4　3

12　13

10　9　14　13

11　6

1

15

First floor

N

0　1　2

1. Front entrance
2. Patio
3. Entrance
4. Corridor
5. Vestibule
6. Bedrooms
7. Living room
8. Study
9. Dining room
10. Living Room.
11. Kitchen
12. Walk-in closet
13. Bathrooms
14. Sauna
15. Garage
16. Storage area
17. Terrace

Photographs: **Stephen Varady** and **Rusell Pell**

Tea Gardens Residence

Stephen Varady Architecture

Collaborator: **Scott Hoy** Construction date: **2000** Location: **Tea Gardens, New South Wales, Australia** Area: **3548 sq. feet**

The Tea Gardens residence sits on a lot filled with trees and shrubs. It is bordered on the south and west by a nature reserve; on the north, by a road; and on the east, by the only neighboring house. The building was carefully placed amid the existing vegetation, on top of a hillock, to take advantage of the views. A wall preserves the privacy of both homes.

From the outset, Stephen Varady envisioned the project as a sculpture. Conceptually, the work consists of a series of walls intersecting a prism on the ground. The north-south walls were painted blue and the east-west walls were painted gray. The largest rooms, such as the living room, kitchen, and dining room, have high ceilings, while the bedrooms have lower ceilings. The high, narrow bathrooms guide the eye toward the outdoors.

The layout of the house is sharply interrupted by a staircase that visually connects the part of the upper floor that faces north with the summer balcony, which faces south.

The design process was influenced by a deep awareness of the ecology, so these spaces are extremely energy-efficient. The windows, for example, are equipped with screens that strategically block the summer sun. The common areas enjoy excellent ventilation, which produces soft, cooling breezes. Finally, the roof can accommodate photovoltaic panels, which will be added when the system becomes more economically viable.

After thorough research, it was decided that the house would be built of concrete, for thermal inertia. Also, concrete is more economical than iron and wood, allowing for coverage of larger areas without significantly increasing the budget. Some of the floors are concrete painted black, and others were covered with strips of wood. The finishing is also wood.

The home is on two levels. The lower-ground floor houses the garage, the rainwater tank, and a storage room; the living quarters are on the upper floor.

One of the architects' goals was to plan a building that would age gracefully. They wanted the walls to be enhanced by age as the weather improved the patina.

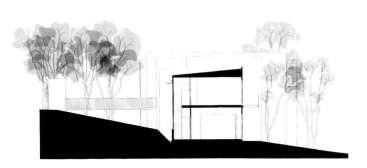

Cross-section

0 1 2

1. Entry hall
2. Bathroom
3. Garage
4. Workshop
5. Water tank
6. Bedrooms
7. Bathroom

8. Balconies
9. Living room
10. Study
11. Dining room
12. Kitchen
13. Bathroom
14. Master bedroom

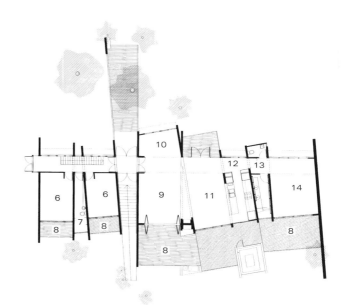

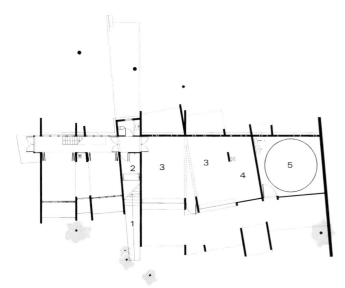

Lower-ground floor

Upper floor

0 1 2

Photographs: **Juan Purcell**

Schmitz House

Felipe Assadi Figueroa

Collaborators: **Jorge Manieu** and **Rodrigo Amunátegui**   Construction date: **2001**   Location: **Calera de Tango, Chile**   Area: **3225 sq. feet**

This house, designed for a couple without children, is located in the midst of an orchard of fruit trees. The plot is located between the Andes and the coastal mountains of Chile, and the nearest views are of lush eucalyptus forests to the north and south. The layout and compositional rhythm of the fruit tree plantings would suggest the optimal placement of the building. Also, the meter-high foliage suggested a new level for the floor so views of the landscape would not be obstructed.

The plan called for a concrete box, a meter high and 2.7 meters wide, facing east-west, that would accommodate the swimming pool and the basement as well as serving

as the foundation of the house. Above it, at treetop height, is the first floor: a glass and larch structure with the common areas occupying a single, diaphanous space, where the only doors hide the bathrooms and a guest room.

The upper level, which is perpendicular to the rest of the grouping, is exposed concrete. As a result of the north-south placement, part of this floor projects outward from the building, casting short shadows on the lower facades.

The different boxes of which the house is constructed were joined together by a common wall. Attached to this wall is the staircase that leads from the basement to the two upper floors. The exposed concrete steps do not touch the walls. This creates a narrow gap in which green lamps were installed to light the way.

The permeability of the structure is in accordance with the amount of privacy required, given the purpose of the different rooms. So, the living room is enclosed entirely in glass, while the master bedroom is mostly opaque.

Thanks to the sunlight, the green glass of the exterior creates colors, transparencies, and reflections which, from the outside, establish a dialogue with the surrounding natural elements. From within, the limits of the space extend to the trees; the space is determined by the immediate surroundings.

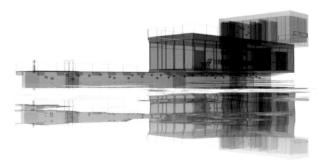

Computer simulations made it possible to visualize the project before it was built, including the effects of the light and the placement of the furniture. Thus, the client and the architect were able to make changes based on a more realistic idea of what the house would be like.

The foundation also serves as retaining walls for the swimming pool. The terrace, which can be used as a diving platform, was covered with dark wooden slats that contrast with the exposed concrete.

The flat terrace on the upper level, which is accessed from the bedroom and study, takes up the entire roof.

The kitchen furnishings consist of two rows of cupboards supported by slender metal poles. Translucent panels between the counter and the upper cupboards help the room blend with the rest of the house. The fact that the cupboards do not extend to the floor or ceiling enhances this effect.

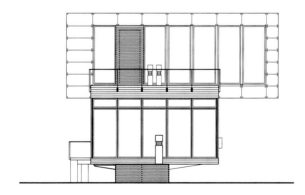

Eastern elevation

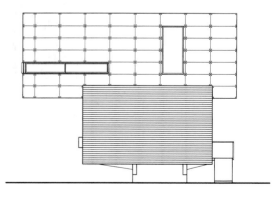

Western elevation

0   1   2

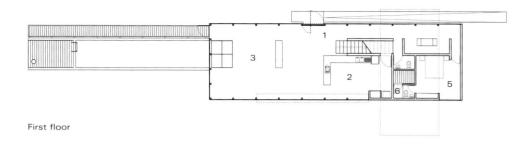

First floor

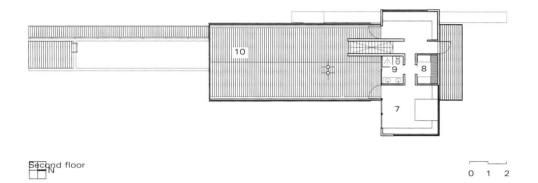

1. Entrance
2. Kitchen
3. Living room
4. Swimming pool
5. Bedroom
6. Lavatories
7. Bedroom
8. Dressing room
9. Bathroom
10. Terrace

Second floor

N

0 1 2

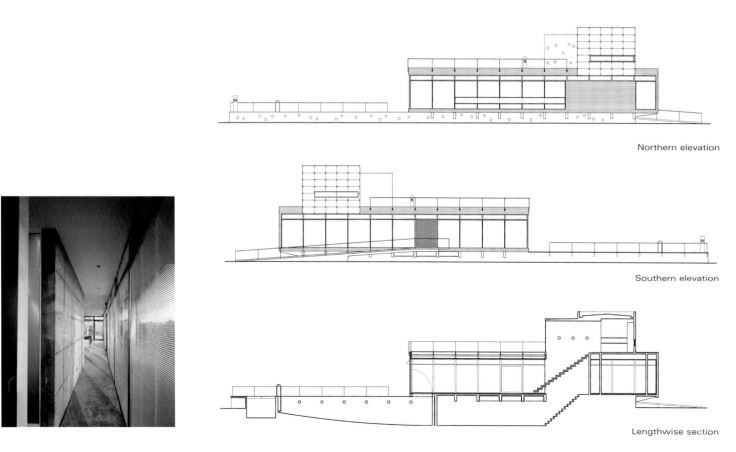

Northern elevation

Southern elevation

Lengthwise section

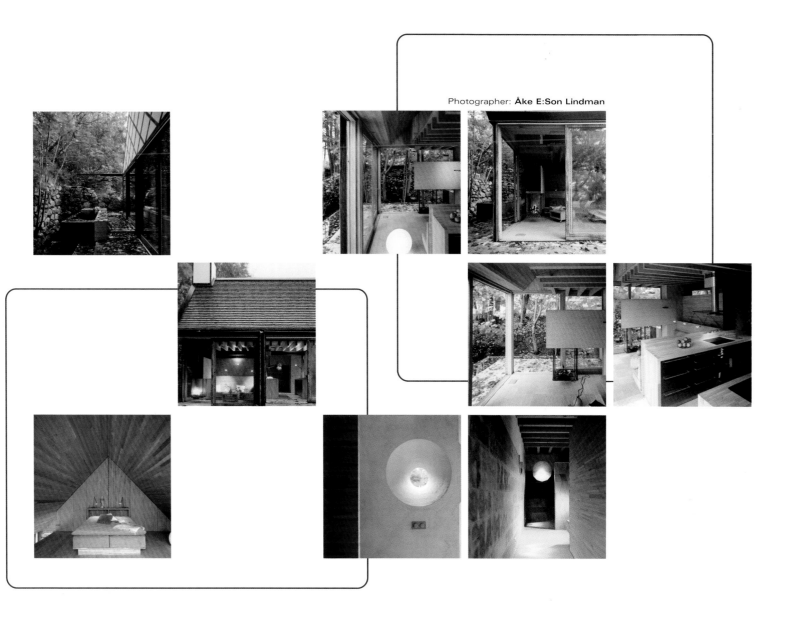

Photographer: Åke E:Son Lindman

Kvarnhuset Villa
Wingårdh Arkitektkontor

Collaborators: **Gunnar Altenhammar** and **Dagon Förvaltnings** Construction date: **2000** Location: **Skåne, Sweden** Area: **1182 sq. feet**

The Kvarnhuset Villa project consisted of converting a mill into a weekend home. The property, originally part of a farm, is in a small town outside Malmö. The various buildings of this rural grouping are located on both banks of a small stream. The house, which is the work of a team headed by Gert Wingardh, is the building nearest the stream and sits on a platform that juts out over the water.

The standard living quarters (living room, kitchen, bedroom, and bathroom) were supplemented with a sauna. Therapeutic rituals like the sauna spawned additional spaces, including a room where users relax before entering the sauna and a swimming pool next to the house for taking cold baths at the end of each session.

The living room, kitchen, bathroom, and sauna are on the first floor. Since it is surrounded by a terrace and closed off by sliding glass doors, the relationship with the exterior is intense, and the house's dominant position is enhanced. The bedroom is in the loft, which is accessed by a stairway at one end of the house. Because of its unusual location, under the sloping roof, it has two triangular walls, one wood and the other glass.

The main construction material is wood, whether boards that form a surface, slats for the sauna steps, or solid pieces that constitute the framework supporting the loft. The furniture, designed by the architects themselves, is also wood. The walls and flooring are concrete and stone, and the exterior walls combine glass with wood trim. The roof is covered by a series of small pieces of slate that evoke the building's agricultural past.

Despite the project's small size, care in the selection of materials and mastery of the construction details have produced a true architectural jewel.

Site plain

Tradition requires that after a session in the sauna one take an icy dip. Since the stream that skirts the property was not big enough, a small swimming pool was installed next to the sauna.

The bedroom is in the loft, a small space under the sloping roof. The northwestern facade has no windows and is finished with the same wood as the floor and ceiling. The southeastern facade is translucent glass with metal trim.

1. Living room
2. Kitchen
3. Bathroom
4. Sauna
5. Bedroom

Second floor

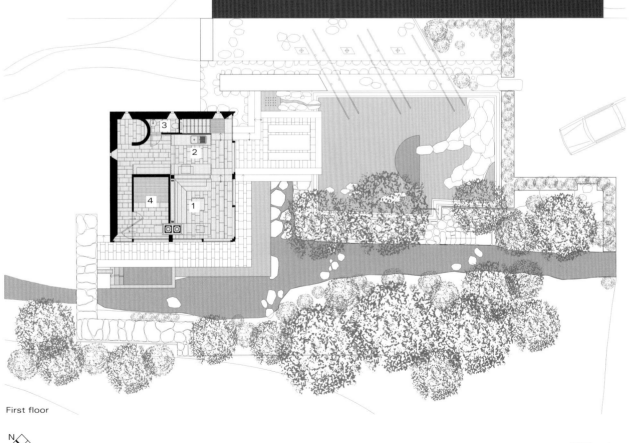

First floor

N

0 1 2

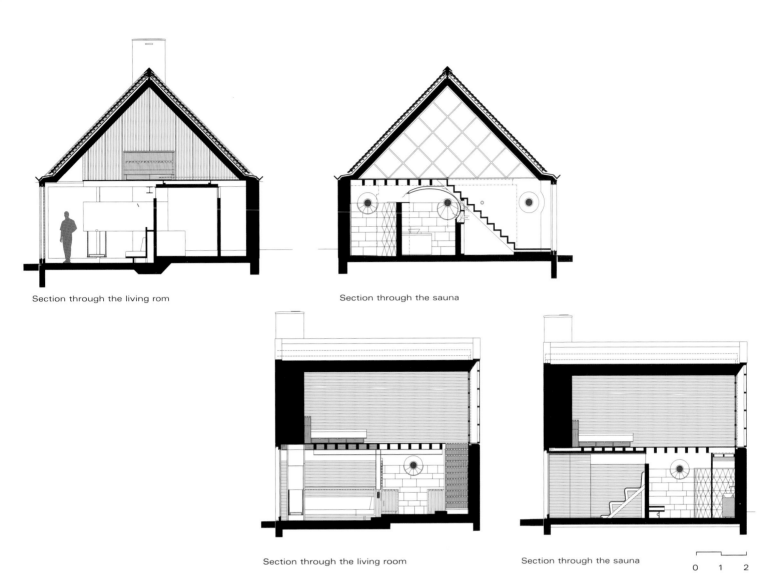

Section through the living rom

Section through the sauna

Section through the living room

Section through the sauna

0   1   2

Photographs: **Peter Kerze**

Jones House

David Salmela

Collaborator: **Souliyahn Keobounpheng**   Construction date: **2000**   Location: **Nerstrand, Southern Minnesota, USA**   Area: **6580 sq.feet**

One of the main concerns of both the clients and the architect was the house's impact on its surroundings, so landscape architects Coen+Stumpf & Associates were hired to make sure the building harmonized with its natural setting.

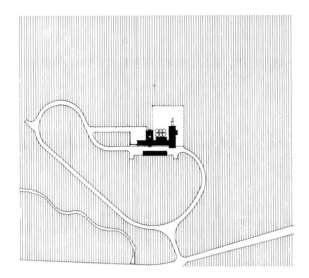

Site Plan

Nowadays, the fabulous American countryside is disappearing, as a result of careless development. This project shows great sensitivity toward its setting, and great commitment to its surroundings.

The clients, who entrusted the project to David Salmela, had always lived in the city until, in their fifties, they decided to leave the hustle and bustle behind, build a house in the country, and become farmers. The main objective was to design a farmstead adapted to the latest agricultural technology yet respectful of a traditional rural setting.

The owners' needs and desires included a granary, guest quarters, a residence, and a garage. All these structures had to be independent, appropriately linked, and optimally positioned to enjoy views of the countryside. Since one of the clients has limited mobility, the entire complex had to be accessible.

The road that guides you onto the farm takes a jog before passing between the garage, which faces north, and the house. The granary is separate from the house, but both structures are covered by the same roof, which marks the limits of a south-facing courtyard.

The house has an L-shaped design. The common areas are found in the long leg.

The couple's bedroom is located in the short leg, which also has a workroom, a swimming pool for therapy, and a laundry room. The cottage, on the other side of the courtyard, contains an office, guest rooms, and rooms for the machinery.

The forms David Salmela chose evoke the structures common to the area and blend

with the countryside. He selected materials frequently used in local construction: brick, echoing the old silos; metal for the roofs and wood, especially cypress and fir. Far from appearing to be nostalgic contrivances, these elements give the complex a rural feel.

The light sources are abundant: floor-to-ceiling windows, sliding doors leading to the courtyard, and small, strategically-placed openings to illuminate some of the rooms.

The interior is finished almost entirely in wood: cypress, pine, and painted plywood.

The kitchen, like the rest of the house, has an old-fashioned feeling to it, evoking traditional rural homes, but it enjoys all the modern conveniences.

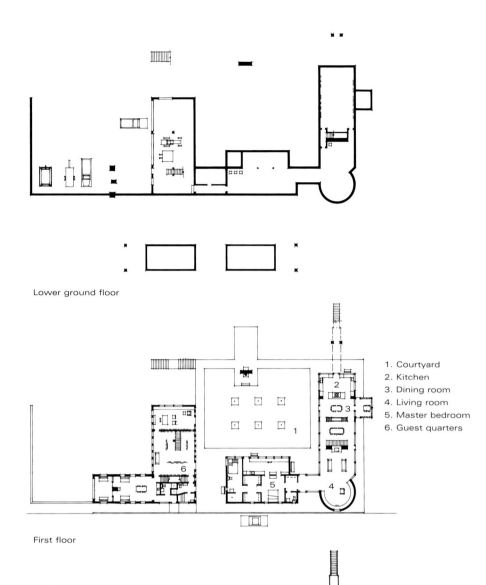

Lower ground floor

1. Courtyard
2. Kitchen
3. Dining room
4. Living room
5. Master bedroom
6. Guest quarters

First floor

Second floor

N

0 1 2

The stairs from the first floor to the loft are wood. Slender panels, painted white, with one end anchored to the framework above and the other to the stair treads, take the place of handrails.

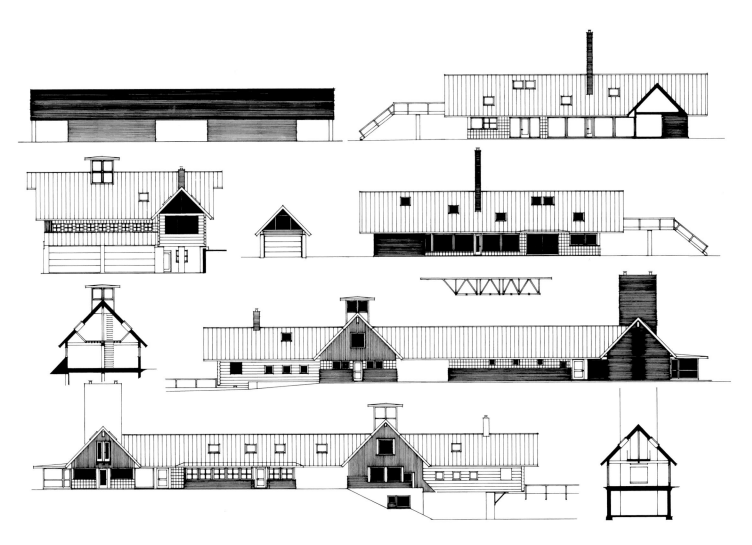

Sections and elevations